AI and Cybersecurity: A Symbiotic Defense System

Artyom Ivanov

About the Author: Artyom Ivanov

Artyom Ivanov is a cybersecurity expert and artificial intelligence enthusiast with over a decade of experience in the intersection of technology and security. With a background in computer science and a deep passion for innovative problem-solving, Artyom has worked with global organizations to develop cutting-edge defense systems that leverage AI to protect against emerging cyber threats. His unique insights blend technical expertise with a strategic understanding of the constantly evolving cybersecurity landscape.

Throughout his career, Artyom has focused on harnessing the power of machine learning, neural networks, and advanced algorithms to enhance security operations and defend critical infrastructure from increasingly sophisticated cyberattacks. He is a sought-after speaker at international tech conferences and has published numerous articles on AI's impact on cybersecurity.

In AI and Cybersecurity: A Symbiotic Defense System, Artyom combines his wealth of knowledge with a forward-looking perspective, exploring the dynamic partnership between AI technologies and cybersecurity. His work not only addresses today's pressing security challenges but also envisions the future of AI-driven defense systems that can adapt, learn, and evolve in real-time.

Artyom Ivanov lives in [insert city/country], where he continues to research the latest advancements in AI and cybersecurity, ensuring that his work stays at the forefront of this rapidly developing field.

In today's hyper-connected world, the digital landscape has become both an incredible asset and a significant vulnerability. As our reliance on technology grows, so does the complexity and sophistication of the cyber threats we face. From ransomware attacks to data breaches and state-sponsored hacking, the scale of cybersecurity challenges is evolving at an alarming rate. Defending against these threats requires more than traditional methods—it demands innovation, intelligence, and adaptability.

This is where Artificial Intelligence (AI) enters the picture. AI is revolutionizing the field of cybersecurity, offering the ability to detect, respond to, and even predict attacks with unprecedented speed and accuracy. The relationship between AI and cybersecurity is symbiotic—AI provides cybersecurity with advanced tools to detect and neutralize threats, while cybersecurity gives AI critical real-world applications that challenge its capabilities and push its development forward.

In **AI and Cybersecurity: A Symbiotic Defense System**, we explore how this powerful partnership is reshaping the way organizations defend against cyber threats. From real-time threat detection and automated incident response to machine learning's role in threat intelligence, this book covers the latest advancements in AI-driven security. We'll delve into practical applications, providing insights into how AI can be leveraged to protect everything from personal devices to global infrastructures. But we'll also address the risks, examining how cybercriminals are beginning to weaponize AI, and the ethical dilemmas posed by its use.

This book is designed to be a comprehensive guide for both cybersecurity professionals and technology enthusiasts looking to understand how AI is transforming digital defense. Each chapter delves into specific aspects of this symbiosis, offering technical insights and real-world examples that demonstrate the profound impact AI is having on cybersecurity.

In the following chapters, you'll discover:

- The foundations of AI and how they are applied in cybersecurity.
- AI's role in automating threat detection, response, and mitigation.
- How adversarial AI is becoming a tool for cybercriminals and the strategies for defending against it.
- The ethical challenges of integrating AI into security systems.

The future of AI in cybersecurity, including predictions for the next wave of technological advancements.

As we face an increasingly uncertain digital future, one thing remains clear: AI will be a critical player in the ongoing battle between security and cybercrime. This book will guide you through that battle, equipping you with the knowledge to not only understand AI's role in cybersecurity but to prepare for what lies ahead.

Welcome to the future of cybersecurity—a future where AI and human expertise work together in harmony, creating a defense system that is smarter, faster, and more resilient than ever before.

Chapter 1: The Cybersecurity Landscape in the Age of AI

As the digital world expands, so do the risks that come with it. In this opening chapter, we explore the evolving cybersecurity landscape, marked by increasingly sophisticated threats and complex attack vectors. From traditional malware to advanced persistent threats (APTs), cybercriminals have become more adaptive, requiring equally adaptive defense mechanisms. This chapter sets the stage for understanding how AI is becoming a critical component in addressing these challenges, transforming cybersecurity from reactive to proactive. By examining current trends and the limitations of conventional security approaches, we lay the foundation for the symbiotic role AI plays in shaping a more resilient digital defense system.

1.1 The Evolution of Cyber Threats: From Viruses to Advanced Persistent Threats (APTs)

The landscape of cyber threats has undergone a dramatic transformation over the past few decades, evolving from simple computer viruses to sophisticated Advanced Persistent Threats (APTs). This evolution reflects the rapid advancements in technology, the growing reliance on digital systems, and the increasing complexity of cybercriminal activities. Understanding this trajectory is essential for developing effective strategies to combat modern cyber threats.

The Early Days: Viruses and Worms

In the early days of computing, cyber threats were relatively simplistic and often motivated by curiosity or a desire to demonstrate technical prowess. The first computer virus, known as the "Creeper," emerged in the early 1970s, spreading from one mainframe computer to another via ARPANET, the precursor to the modern internet. However, it was the 1980s and 1990s that saw a surge in the proliferation of viruses, worms, and trojans.

Viruses, which attach themselves to legitimate programs or files, would replicate themselves and spread from one system to another. Notable examples include the "Melissa" virus, which spread via infected email attachments, and the "ILOVEYOU" worm, which wreaked havoc globally by enticing users to open an innocuous email. These early threats were typically not designed for financial gain but rather to disrupt systems or spread for the sake of spreading.

The introduction of antivirus software during this period marked the beginning of a cat-and-mouse game between cybersecurity professionals and cybercriminals. Antivirus programs became essential tools in the fight against these primitive threats, enabling users to detect and remove malicious software. However, the basic nature of these threats meant they could often be contained and eliminated without significant long-term damage.

The Rise of Malware: Trojans, Spyware, and Adware

As the internet became more accessible in the late 1990s and early 2000s, the landscape of cyber threats began to evolve. Cybercriminals started to develop more complex forms of malware, such as trojans, spyware, and adware, which targeted users for financial gain. Unlike traditional viruses, these types of malware often operated covertly, making it harder for users to detect their presence.

Trojans masquerade as legitimate software but carry hidden malicious code. They could be used to create backdoors into infected systems, allowing attackers to steal sensitive information or gain control over the machine. Spyware was designed to monitor users' activities without their knowledge, capturing keystrokes and collecting personal information, such as login credentials and financial data. Adware generated revenue for cybercriminals by forcing users to view unwanted advertisements, often compromising system performance in the process.

This shift marked a transition from cyber threats that were disruptive to threats that were financially motivated. Cybercriminals began to realize the profitability of targeting individuals and organizations for monetary gain, leading to the emergence of organized cybercrime groups.

The Emergence of Botnets and DDoS Attacks

As cyber threats evolved, so did the tactics used by cybercriminals. The early 2000s saw the rise of botnets—networks of compromised computers controlled by a central command. Cybercriminals would infect thousands of devices with malware, turning them into "zombie" machines that could be used to launch Distributed Denial of Service (DDoS) attacks.

DDoS attacks overwhelm a targeted server, service, or network with a flood of internet traffic, rendering it unusable. These attacks could be politically motivated, aimed at silencing dissent or activism, or financially motivated, intended to extort companies by threatening to disrupt their services. High-profile DDoS attacks, such as the one on the banking sector in 2012, demonstrated the potential for widespread damage and disruption, highlighting the need for more robust cybersecurity measures.

The Advent of APTs: Targeted and Sustained Attacks

With the rise of sophisticated cybercriminal organizations and state-sponsored hacking groups, the cybersecurity landscape underwent another transformation with the emergence of Advanced Persistent Threats (APTs). APTs are characterized by their targeted and sustained nature, often aimed at specific organizations, government agencies, or critical infrastructure.

Unlike earlier cyber threats, which often relied on indiscriminate methods of spreading, APTs are meticulously planned and executed. Attackers typically conduct extensive reconnaissance to identify vulnerabilities within their targets, often utilizing social engineering techniques to gain access. Once inside the network, they can remain undetected for extended periods, allowing them to gather sensitive information, exfiltrate data, or manipulate systems at will.

One of the most notorious examples of an APT is the "Stuxnet" worm, discovered in 2010. Believed to be developed by the U.S. and Israel, Stuxnet was specifically designed to target Iran's nuclear facilities, sabotaging equipment while making it appear as though nothing had happened. This marked a significant shift in the nature of cyber warfare, demonstrating that cyberattacks could be used to achieve strategic objectives without traditional military engagement.

APTs can involve multiple phases, including initial intrusion, lateral movement within a network, data collection, and exfiltration. The complexity and stealth of these attacks require a proactive and multilayered defense strategy, making traditional cybersecurity measures inadequate.

The Current Threat Landscape: Evolving Tactics and Techniques

Today, the threat landscape continues to evolve, with cybercriminals adopting new tactics, techniques, and procedures (TTPs) to evade detection and maximize their impact. Ransomware attacks, for example, have surged in popularity, with attackers encrypting victims' data and demanding a ransom for its release. High-profile attacks, such as the Colonial Pipeline incident in 2021, illustrate the potential for ransomware to disrupt critical infrastructure and instill fear in organizations.

Cyber threats have also become more sophisticated through the use of artificial intelligence and machine learning. Attackers can now develop automated tools to exploit vulnerabilities, bypass security measures, and scale their operations. This has led to an increase in the volume of attacks, as well as a diversification of targets, including small businesses, healthcare organizations, and educational institutions.

The Future of Cyber Threats: Preparing for the Unknown

As technology continues to advance, the evolution of cyber threats is likely to continue, presenting new challenges for individuals and organizations alike. Emerging technologies, such as the Internet of Things (IoT) and 5G networks, introduce new vulnerabilities that cybercriminals can exploit. As more devices become interconnected, the potential attack surface expands, requiring a reevaluation of traditional cybersecurity practices.

The ongoing arms race between cybercriminals and defenders emphasizes the need for continuous adaptation and improvement of cybersecurity strategies. Organizations must invest in advanced security solutions, threat intelligence, and employee training to stay ahead of evolving threats. Collaboration between the public and private sectors will be essential in developing a comprehensive approach to cybersecurity that addresses both current and future challenges.

The evolution of cyber threats from simple viruses to advanced persistent threats underscores the complexity of the cybersecurity landscape. As technology advances, so too do the tactics employed by cybercriminals, necessitating a proactive and adaptive approach to cybersecurity. Understanding this evolution is crucial for developing effective strategies to combat modern threats and safeguarding sensitive information in an increasingly interconnected world. By acknowledging the lessons of the past and preparing for the uncertainties of the future, organizations can strengthen their defenses and navigate the ever-changing landscape of cyber threats.

1.2 Cybersecurity Challenges in a Hyper-Connected World

In today's digital age, the proliferation of connected devices, cloud services, and the Internet of Things (IoT) has ushered in a hyper-connected world, transforming how individuals and organizations interact, communicate, and conduct business. While these advancements offer significant benefits, they also present a myriad of cybersecurity challenges that demand urgent attention and innovative solutions. Understanding these challenges is essential for developing effective strategies to safeguard sensitive information and maintain trust in an increasingly interconnected environment.

1. Expanding Attack Surface

One of the most significant challenges posed by a hyper-connected world is the expanding attack surface. As organizations adopt more connected devices and systems, each new endpoint introduces potential vulnerabilities that cybercriminals can exploit. The IoT, in particular, has seen explosive growth, with billions of devices now interconnected—ranging from smart home appliances to industrial sensors. Many of these devices were designed with convenience in mind, often sacrificing security for ease of use.

With such a vast number of connected devices, attackers can target weak links in the network, taking advantage of insufficient security measures to gain unauthorized access. For instance, a compromised IoT device can serve as a foothold for attackers, allowing them to move laterally within a network and access sensitive data or critical infrastructure.

2. Data Privacy and Protection

As more personal and organizational data is generated and shared across interconnected platforms, ensuring data privacy and protection has become increasingly challenging. The collection of vast amounts of data, often referred to as "big data," has enabled businesses to gain valuable insights into customer behavior and operational efficiencies. However, this data also poses significant risks if not properly secured.

In a hyper-connected environment, sensitive information can be transmitted across multiple channels and stored in various locations, increasing the likelihood of data breaches. Cybercriminals are constantly devising new tactics to steal personal information, including phishing attacks and exploiting vulnerabilities in applications and cloud services. High-profile data breaches have demonstrated the severe consequences of inadequate data protection, leading to regulatory scrutiny, loss of customer trust, and substantial financial losses.

3. Complexity of Security Management

The interconnected nature of modern networks introduces complexity into security management. Organizations often deploy a diverse array of devices, applications, and platforms, each with its own security protocols and requirements. This complexity can make it challenging to maintain a unified security strategy, resulting in potential gaps in protection.

Moreover, many organizations struggle with integrating legacy systems with newer technologies, leading to inconsistencies in security measures. The lack of standardized security protocols across different devices and platforms further complicates efforts to establish comprehensive security frameworks. As a result, organizations may find it difficult to monitor and respond to threats effectively, increasing their vulnerability to cyberattacks.

4. Insider Threats and Human Error

While external cyber threats receive much attention, insider threats—whether intentional or unintentional—pose significant risks in a hyper-connected world. Employees, contractors, and third-party vendors often have access to sensitive information and systems, making them potential sources of security breaches.

Human error is another critical factor contributing to cybersecurity challenges. Employees may inadvertently expose organizations to risk by falling victim to phishing attacks, misconfiguring security settings, or neglecting to follow established protocols. In a hyper-connected environment, the consequences of such errors can be magnified, leading to widespread repercussions for the organization and its customers.

5. Evolving Threat Landscape

The rapid pace of technological advancement means that the threat landscape is constantly evolving. Cybercriminals are continually adapting their tactics, techniques, and procedures to exploit new vulnerabilities and evade detection. This evolving nature of threats complicates efforts to establish effective defense strategies.

For example, as organizations increasingly adopt artificial intelligence (AI) and machine learning (ML) technologies, cybercriminals are also utilizing these tools to automate attacks and enhance their effectiveness. Ransomware attacks have become more sophisticated, with attackers employing advanced techniques to encrypt files and demand ransoms. The rise of state-sponsored cyber activities has also introduced new dimensions to the threat landscape, with politically motivated attacks targeting critical infrastructure and sensitive data.

6. Regulatory Compliance and Legal Challenges

As cyber threats continue to grow, so do the regulatory and legal requirements governing data protection and cybersecurity. Organizations must navigate a complex landscape of regulations, including the General Data Protection Regulation (GDPR), the Health Insurance Portability and Accountability Act (HIPAA), and various industry-specific standards. Non-compliance can result in severe penalties and legal repercussions.

In a hyper-connected world, ensuring compliance becomes more challenging as data crosses international borders and involves multiple stakeholders. Organizations must implement comprehensive data governance and compliance strategies to safeguard sensitive information and mitigate legal risks. Failure to do so can result in reputational damage, loss of customer trust, and significant financial consequences.

7. Third-Party Risks

The interconnected nature of modern business ecosystems often involves collaboration with third-party vendors and service providers. While these partnerships can enhance operational efficiency, they also introduce additional cybersecurity risks. A breach at a third-party vendor can have cascading effects, compromising the security of connected organizations.

Organizations must assess the security posture of their vendors and establish robust vendor management processes to mitigate these risks. This includes conducting thorough due diligence, implementing contractual security requirements, and continuously monitoring third-party security practices. Inadequate oversight of third-party vendors can leave organizations vulnerable to supply chain attacks and data breaches.

8. The Skills Gap in Cybersecurity

The demand for cybersecurity professionals continues to outpace supply, leading to a significant skills gap in the industry. As organizations navigate the complexities of a hyper-connected world, the need for skilled cybersecurity experts has never been greater. However, the lack of qualified professionals poses challenges for organizations attempting to implement effective security measures.

To address this skills gap, organizations must invest in training and development programs to upskill their existing workforce. Collaborating with educational institutions and industry organizations can also help cultivate a pipeline of talent. Bridging the skills gap is essential for ensuring that organizations are adequately equipped to defend against evolving cyber threats.

Navigating the cybersecurity challenges of a hyper-connected world requires a proactive and multifaceted approach. Organizations must adopt comprehensive security strategies that address the expanding attack surface, protect sensitive data, and manage the complexities of interconnected systems. By fostering a culture of security awareness, investing in advanced technologies, and prioritizing collaboration, organizations can better prepare themselves to face the evolving landscape of cyber threats.

In this digital era, the stakes have never been higher, and organizations must remain vigilant in their efforts to safeguard their assets and maintain the trust of their customers. As the world becomes increasingly interconnected, the responsibility of securing the digital landscape rests on the shoulders of every organization and individual. Only through concerted efforts and a commitment to continuous improvement can we hope to address the cybersecurity challenges of our hyper-connected reality.

1.3 The Rise of AI in Digital Defense

The landscape of cybersecurity is undergoing a revolutionary transformation driven by the integration of artificial intelligence (AI) technologies. As cyber threats grow more sophisticated and pervasive, organizations are increasingly turning to AI to bolster their digital defenses. This chapter explores the rise of AI in digital defense, examining its key applications, benefits, challenges, and future prospects.

1. The Necessity of AI in Cybersecurity

The rapid evolution of cyber threats—from viruses and malware to advanced persistent threats (APTs)—has created an urgent need for innovative cybersecurity solutions. Traditional security measures often struggle to keep pace with the growing complexity and volume of attacks. In this context, AI emerges as a vital tool capable of enhancing threat detection, response, and mitigation.

One of the primary drivers behind the adoption of AI in cybersecurity is the sheer volume of data generated in modern digital environments. Organizations are inundated with vast amounts of security data from various sources, including network traffic, user behavior, and endpoint devices. Analyzing this data manually is not only time-consuming but also prone to human error. AI algorithms, particularly machine learning (ML) models, can sift through this data at unprecedented speeds, identifying patterns and anomalies that may indicate potential threats.

2. Key Applications of AI in Digital Defense

AI is being leveraged across various domains within cybersecurity, each application enhancing an organization's ability to defend against cyber threats.

a. Threat Detection and Prevention

AI-driven systems can detect threats more effectively than traditional methods by utilizing machine learning algorithms that continuously learn and adapt. These systems can analyze historical data and real-time network traffic to identify unusual patterns that may signify a cyberattack. For example, AI can identify deviations in user behavior, such as a sudden increase in data downloads or access to restricted areas, alerting security teams to potential insider threats or compromised accounts.

b. Automated Incident Response

AI not only aids in detecting threats but also plays a crucial role in automating incident response. AI-powered systems can rapidly execute predefined response protocols, such as isolating compromised devices, blocking malicious IP addresses, or rolling back unauthorized changes. By automating these processes, organizations can significantly reduce response times and minimize the impact of cyber incidents. This capability is especially valuable in the context of ransomware attacks, where swift action can prevent data loss and mitigate damage.

c. Security Orchestration and Threat Intelligence

AI can enhance security orchestration by integrating data from multiple security tools and platforms. This unified approach allows organizations to correlate information from various sources, providing a comprehensive view of the security landscape. AI-driven threat intelligence platforms can analyze global threat data, identifying emerging trends and vulnerabilities that may impact an organization. By staying ahead of potential threats, organizations can proactively strengthen their defenses and mitigate risks.

d. Behavioral Analysis and User Authentication

AI technologies are also employed in behavioral analysis, which helps organizations monitor user activity and identify anomalous behavior. By establishing baseline behavior patterns for users, AI can detect deviations that may indicate compromised accounts or insider threats. This capability enhances user authentication processes, allowing organizations to implement adaptive security measures, such as multi-factor authentication, based on real-time risk assessments.

3. Benefits of AI in Digital Defense

The integration of AI in digital defense offers numerous advantages that enhance an organization's cybersecurity posture.

a. Enhanced Speed and Accuracy

AI systems can analyze vast amounts of data in real-time, identifying threats more quickly and accurately than human analysts. This speed enables organizations to respond to potential threats proactively, significantly reducing the window of opportunity for attackers.

b. Scalability

As organizations expand their digital footprints, the need for scalable security solutions becomes paramount. AI can adapt to the growing volume of data and devices, providing consistent protection without requiring proportional increases in human resources. This scalability is essential for organizations navigating the complexities of cloud environments and IoT deployments.

c. Cost Efficiency

By automating routine security tasks and reducing the reliance on manual analysis, AI can lead to cost savings for organizations. Security teams can focus on higher-level strategic initiatives and complex investigations, maximizing the value of their expertise while minimizing operational costs.

d. Improved Threat Prediction

AI systems can analyze historical threat data to identify trends and predict future attacks. This predictive capability enables organizations to take preemptive measures, such as patching vulnerabilities or enhancing security protocols, before threats materialize.

4. Challenges and Limitations of AI in Cybersecurity

Despite its significant advantages, the integration of AI in digital defense also presents challenges that organizations must address.

a. Data Quality and Bias

AI algorithms rely on high-quality data to function effectively. If the training data is biased or incomplete, it can lead to inaccurate predictions and poor threat detection. Organizations must ensure they are using diverse and representative datasets to train AI models, mitigating the risk of bias and enhancing the system's effectiveness.

b. Adversarial Attacks

As AI technologies advance, so do the tactics employed by cybercriminals. Adversarial attacks specifically target AI models, seeking to manipulate their outputs or confuse them. For example, attackers can introduce subtle changes to input data to mislead AI-driven threat detection systems. Organizations must develop robust defenses against adversarial tactics to safeguard their AI systems.

c. Integration Challenges

Integrating AI solutions into existing security frameworks can be complex. Organizations may face challenges in aligning new AI tools with legacy systems, requiring careful planning and execution. Successful integration often involves reevaluating workflows, security protocols, and personnel training.

d. Trust and Transparency

AI decision-making processes can be opaque, leading to concerns about trust and accountability. Security teams may find it challenging to understand why an AI system flagged a particular behavior as malicious. Enhancing the transparency of AI algorithms and providing explanations for their decisions is crucial for building trust among security professionals.

5. The Future of AI in Digital Defense

The rise of AI in digital defense represents a paradigm shift in how organizations approach cybersecurity. As technology continues to evolve, we can expect further advancements in AI capabilities and applications. Emerging trends such as explainable AI, which aims to make AI decision-making more transparent, will play a critical role in building trust and facilitating broader adoption within the cybersecurity community.

Furthermore, as the threat landscape becomes increasingly complex, AI will likely play a central role in enhancing the resilience of organizations against cyberattacks. By continuously learning and adapting to new threats, AI systems can provide dynamic defenses that evolve in real-time.

The rise of AI in digital defense signifies a crucial turning point in the battle against cyber threats. By leveraging AI technologies, organizations can enhance their threat detection, response, and mitigation capabilities, ultimately strengthening their overall cybersecurity posture. While challenges remain, the potential benefits of AI are immense, providing organizations with the tools they need to navigate the complexities of a hyper-connected world. As we look to the future, the collaboration between AI and cybersecurity will undoubtedly shape the next generation of digital defense strategies, fostering a more secure digital landscape for all.

Chapter 2: Foundations of Artificial Intelligence in Cybersecurity

In this chapter, we delve into the core principles of artificial intelligence and how they are applied in the realm of cybersecurity. We begin by exploring the fundamentals of AI, including machine learning, deep learning, and neural networks, explaining how these technologies empower systems to analyze vast amounts of data and recognize complex patterns. We then examine the specific AI algorithms most commonly used to enhance cybersecurity, from anomaly detection to predictive analytics. By building a solid understanding of AI's foundational technologies, this chapter prepares you to see how these tools are integrated into real-world cybersecurity solutions, setting the stage for more advanced discussions on AI-driven defenses.

2.1 Understanding the Basics of Machine Learning and Deep Learning

In the realm of artificial intelligence (AI), two key subfields—machine learning (ML) and deep learning (DL)—are revolutionizing how we process data, recognize patterns, and make predictions. Understanding the fundamentals of these technologies is essential for appreciating their applications in cybersecurity and other domains. This section provides an overview of machine learning and deep learning, elucidating their core principles, methodologies, and distinctions.

1. Defining Machine Learning

Machine learning is a branch of AI that focuses on the development of algorithms and statistical models that enable computers to perform tasks without explicit instructions. Instead of following predetermined rules, machine learning systems learn from data, allowing them to identify patterns and make decisions based on input.

a. Types of Machine Learning

Machine learning can be broadly categorized into three types:

Supervised Learning: In supervised learning, the model is trained on a labeled dataset, meaning that each training example is paired with the correct output. The objective is to learn a mapping from input features to output labels, allowing the model to make predictions on new, unseen data. Common applications of supervised learning include spam detection, image classification, and regression analysis.

Unsupervised Learning: Unsupervised learning involves training a model on an unlabeled dataset, where the algorithm must identify patterns and relationships within the data without guidance. Common techniques include clustering (grouping similar data points) and dimensionality reduction (reducing the number of features while retaining important information). Unsupervised learning is often used for customer segmentation, anomaly detection, and exploratory data analysis.

Reinforcement Learning: Reinforcement learning is a type of learning where an agent interacts with an environment, receiving feedback in the form of rewards or penalties. The goal is to learn a policy that maximizes cumulative rewards over time. This approach is commonly used in robotics, game playing (e.g., AlphaGo), and automated decision-making systems.

2. The Role of Algorithms in Machine Learning

At the core of machine learning are algorithms—mathematical models that process data to learn from it. Some popular algorithms include:

Linear Regression: A statistical method used for predicting a continuous outcome based on one or more predictor variables. It assumes a linear relationship between the variables.

Decision Trees: A model that uses a tree-like structure to make decisions based on feature values. Each internal node represents a feature, each branch represents a decision rule, and each leaf node represents an outcome.

Support Vector Machines (SVM): An algorithm that finds the optimal hyperplane to separate different classes in the feature space. SVMs are particularly effective for high-dimensional data.

k-Nearest Neighbors (k-NN): A simple algorithm that classifies a data point based on the majority class of its k nearest neighbors in the feature space.

3. Introduction to Deep Learning

Deep learning is a specialized subset of machine learning that focuses on neural networks—models inspired by the structure and function of the human brain. These networks consist of multiple layers of interconnected nodes (neurons) that process data in a hierarchical manner.

a. Neural Networks

At the heart of deep learning is the neural network, which is designed to recognize patterns and relationships in data. A typical neural network consists of three main components:

Input Layer: The layer that receives input data, where each node represents a feature of the data.

Hidden Layers: One or more layers between the input and output layers, where complex computations occur. Each hidden layer consists of numerous neurons that transform the input data through weighted connections.

Output Layer: The final layer that produces the output, which can be a classification label, a predicted value, or a probability distribution.

b. Activation Functions

Neural networks utilize activation functions to introduce non-linearity into the model, allowing it to learn complex patterns. Common activation functions include:

Sigmoid: Produces outputs between 0 and 1, often used in binary classification.

ReLU (Rectified Linear Unit): Allows only positive values to pass through, enabling faster training and reducing the likelihood of vanishing gradients.

Softmax: Converts the output of a neural network into a probability distribution, commonly used in multi-class classification tasks.

4. Training Machine Learning and Deep Learning Models

The process of training machine learning and deep learning models involves several key steps:

Data Preparation: Collecting, cleaning, and preprocessing the data to ensure it is suitable for analysis. This may involve handling missing values, normalizing data, and encoding categorical variables.

Model Selection: Choosing an appropriate algorithm or model based on the problem at hand, such as classification, regression, or clustering.

Training: Feeding the prepared data into the model to learn patterns. During this phase, the model adjusts its internal parameters (weights) to minimize the difference between predicted and actual outputs, typically using a technique called gradient descent.

Validation: Evaluating the model's performance on a separate validation dataset to assess its ability to generalize to unseen data. Techniques such as cross-validation can be employed to ensure robustness.

Testing: Once the model has been validated, it is tested on a distinct test dataset to measure its performance metrics, such as accuracy, precision, recall, and F1-score.

5. Differences Between Machine Learning and Deep Learning

While both machine learning and deep learning are powerful techniques for data analysis, there are key differences between them:

Data Requirements: Deep learning models typically require larger datasets to achieve optimal performance due to their complexity, while traditional machine learning algorithms can perform well with smaller datasets.

Feature Engineering: In traditional machine learning, feature engineering (the process of selecting and transforming input variables) is often necessary to improve model performance. In contrast, deep learning models can automatically extract relevant features from raw data, reducing the need for manual intervention.

Computational Resources: Deep learning models are computationally intensive and often require specialized hardware, such as Graphics Processing Units (GPUs), for efficient training. Machine learning algorithms, on the other hand, can often be trained on standard hardware.

Interpretability: Machine learning models, particularly simpler algorithms like decision trees or linear regression, tend to be more interpretable than deep learning models, which are often seen as "black boxes." Understanding how deep learning models make decisions can be challenging, raising concerns in critical applications where transparency is essential.

6. Applications in Cybersecurity

Machine learning and deep learning have found numerous applications in cybersecurity, enhancing threat detection, incident response, and risk management. Some key applications include:

Intrusion Detection Systems (IDS): Machine learning algorithms can analyze network traffic patterns to identify unusual behavior indicative of a cyberattack, enabling early detection and response.

Malware Classification: Deep learning models can analyze file characteristics to classify malware variants, helping organizations protect against evolving threats.

Phishing Detection: Natural language processing (NLP) techniques, combined with machine learning, can analyze email content and metadata to identify potential phishing attempts.

User Behavior Analytics: Machine learning algorithms can establish baseline behavior patterns for users, flagging anomalous activities that may indicate compromised accounts or insider threats.

Understanding the basics of machine learning and deep learning is essential for appreciating their transformative impact on cybersecurity and other fields. By leveraging these technologies, organizations can enhance their ability to detect, respond to, and mitigate cyber threats. As machine learning and deep learning continue to evolve, they will play an increasingly pivotal role in shaping the future of digital defense, enabling organizations to stay ahead of emerging threats in a rapidly changing landscape.

2.2 Key AI Algorithms for Cybersecurity Applications

The integration of artificial intelligence (AI) into cybersecurity is revolutionizing how organizations detect, respond to, and mitigate threats. AI algorithms provide advanced capabilities for analyzing vast amounts of data, identifying patterns, and making informed decisions based on those patterns. This section discusses key AI algorithms that are particularly relevant for cybersecurity applications, highlighting their functionalities, advantages, and practical use cases.

1. Supervised Learning Algorithms

Supervised learning algorithms are foundational to many AI applications in cybersecurity. They learn from labeled datasets, where each data point is paired with an output label. These algorithms excel in tasks such as classification and regression.

a. Decision Trees

Description: Decision trees are a flowchart-like model that makes decisions based on feature values. Each internal node represents a feature, each branch indicates a decision rule, and each leaf node represents an outcome (e.g., "malicious" or "benign").

Advantages: Decision trees are easy to interpret and visualize, making them accessible for security analysts. They also handle both categorical and numerical data well.

Use Cases: Commonly used for malware classification and intrusion detection. For example, decision trees can analyze network traffic patterns and classify them as normal or anomalous based on defined thresholds.

b. Support Vector Machines (SVM)

Description: Support Vector Machines are classification algorithms that find the optimal hyperplane to separate different classes in a feature space. The algorithm focuses on maximizing the margin between data points from different classes.

Advantages: SVMs are effective in high-dimensional spaces and are robust to overfitting, especially in cases where the number of dimensions exceeds the number of samples.

Use Cases: SVMs can be employed for spam detection and malware classification, where they learn to differentiate between malicious and benign files based on their features.

c. Random Forest

Description: Random Forest is an ensemble learning method that constructs multiple decision trees and aggregates their predictions. Each tree is trained on a random subset of the data, enhancing model robustness and accuracy.

Advantages: This algorithm reduces the risk of overfitting compared to a single decision tree and is effective for both classification and regression tasks.

Use Cases: Frequently used in anomaly detection, such as identifying unauthorized access attempts in network logs by combining predictions from multiple decision trees.

2. Unsupervised Learning Algorithms

Unsupervised learning algorithms do not require labeled data and are adept at finding hidden patterns or intrinsic structures in the data. These algorithms are particularly useful for tasks like clustering and anomaly detection.

a. K-Means Clustering

Description: K-Means is a clustering algorithm that partitions data into K distinct clusters based on feature similarity. It iteratively assigns data points to the nearest cluster centroid and updates the centroids until convergence.

Advantages: K-Means is computationally efficient and easy to implement, making it a popular choice for exploratory data analysis.

Use Cases: Employed for user behavior analysis, where it groups users with similar behavior patterns to identify potential insider threats or account compromises.

b. Isolation Forest

Description: Isolation Forest is an anomaly detection algorithm that identifies outliers by randomly partitioning data points. It isolates observations by creating random trees and measures how many splits it takes to isolate a point.

Advantages: This algorithm is particularly effective for high-dimensional data and can handle large datasets efficiently.

Use Cases: Used to detect intrusions in network traffic by identifying unusual patterns that deviate from normal behavior.

c. Principal Component Analysis (PCA)

Description: PCA is a dimensionality reduction technique that transforms high-dimensional data into a lower-dimensional space while retaining as much variance as possible. It identifies the principal components that capture the most information.

Advantages: PCA helps reduce noise in the data and improves the performance of other machine learning algorithms.

Use Cases: Utilized for reducing the feature space in cybersecurity datasets, enhancing the performance of supervised learning models for tasks like intrusion detection.

3. Deep Learning Algorithms

Deep learning algorithms are designed to process data through multiple layers of neural networks. They are particularly powerful in handling unstructured data, such as images, audio, and text.

a. Convolutional Neural Networks (CNNs)

Description: CNNs are specialized neural networks primarily used for processing grid-like data, such as images. They utilize convolutional layers to automatically extract features from input data, reducing the need for manual feature extraction.

Advantages: CNNs excel at recognizing patterns and are highly effective for image-based tasks.

Use Cases: Employed in malware detection, where they analyze file images or network packet captures to identify malicious content.

b. Recurrent Neural Networks (RNNs)

Description: RNNs are designed for processing sequential data, allowing information to persist across sequences. They use feedback loops to maintain information about previous inputs, making them ideal for time-series data.

Advantages: RNNs are effective for modeling sequences and have been widely adopted in natural language processing tasks.

Use Cases: Used for detecting phishing attacks in emails by analyzing the sequential nature of text and identifying malicious patterns.

c. Long Short-Term Memory (LSTM) Networks

Description: LSTMs are a type of RNN that addresses the vanishing gradient problem by using specialized memory cells. They can learn long-term dependencies in sequential data.

Advantages: LSTMs are particularly well-suited for tasks requiring context understanding over extended sequences.

Use Cases: Applied in detecting anomalies in network traffic patterns over time, identifying unusual spikes or drops in activity that could indicate an attack.

4. Reinforcement Learning Algorithms

Reinforcement learning (RL) involves training an agent to make decisions based on feedback from its environment. The agent learns to maximize rewards by exploring different actions.

a. Q-Learning

Description: Q-Learning is a model-free reinforcement learning algorithm that learns a policy mapping states to actions by estimating the value of action-reward pairs.

Advantages: It does not require a model of the environment and can learn optimal policies in dynamic settings.

Use Cases: Used in automated incident response systems, where an RL agent learns to make decisions about containment or remediation actions based on feedback from previous incidents.

b. Deep Q-Networks (DQN)

Description: DQNs combine Q-Learning with deep learning techniques. They use neural networks to approximate the Q-value function, enabling the agent to handle high-dimensional state spaces.

Advantages: DQNs can learn complex policies in environments with rich observations.

Use Cases: Employed in real-time decision-making scenarios, such as automatically adjusting security settings based on ongoing threat assessments.

The application of AI algorithms in cybersecurity is transforming how organizations approach threat detection and response. By leveraging machine learning, deep learning, and reinforcement learning techniques, organizations can enhance their ability to identify, analyze, and mitigate cyber threats. Each algorithm offers unique strengths and is suited to specific use cases, emphasizing the need for a multi-faceted approach to cybersecurity.

As cyber threats continue to evolve in complexity and frequency, the importance of adopting advanced AI algorithms will only grow. By integrating these technologies into their cybersecurity frameworks, organizations can stay ahead of emerging threats and protect their digital assets more effectively.

2.3 Real-World Examples of AI-Enhanced Cyber Defense Systems

The integration of artificial intelligence (AI) into cybersecurity has led to the development of innovative defense systems that enhance threat detection, response, and mitigation strategies. These AI-enhanced cyber defense systems have been successfully implemented across various industries, demonstrating their effectiveness in combating an increasingly sophisticated array of cyber threats. This section highlights several notable real-world examples, showcasing how organizations leverage AI technologies to bolster their cybersecurity posture.

1. Darktrace: Autonomous Response Technology

Overview: Darktrace is a leading cybersecurity company known for its application of AI and machine learning to detect and respond to cyber threats in real-time. Its Autonomous Response technology enables organizations to autonomously respond to emerging threats without human intervention.

Key Features:

- **Self-Learning AI**: Darktrace's AI technology utilizes unsupervised machine learning algorithms to analyze network traffic patterns, establishing a baseline of normal behavior. This enables the system to detect anomalies that may indicate potential cyber threats.

- **Threat Visualization**: The system provides a graphical interface that visualizes the network and highlights areas of concern, allowing security teams to quickly identify and investigate suspicious activities.
- **Autonomous Response**: In the event of a detected threat, Darktrace can automatically initiate a response by isolating affected devices or restricting access, thereby minimizing potential damage.
- **Real-World Impact**: Organizations using Darktrace have reported a significant reduction in the time taken to detect and respond to threats. The autonomous capabilities of the system allow for quicker remediation, ultimately enhancing overall security and reducing the likelihood of successful attacks.

2. CrowdStrike: Falcon Platform

Overview: CrowdStrike is a cybersecurity company that provides a cloud-native endpoint protection platform called Falcon. This platform leverages AI and machine learning to deliver comprehensive protection against various cyber threats.

Key Features:

- **Real-Time Threat Intelligence**: The Falcon platform continuously monitors endpoints for signs of malicious activity, utilizing AI algorithms to analyze behavioral patterns and identify threats in real-time.
- **Threat Hunting**: The platform offers proactive threat hunting capabilities, enabling security teams to search for indicators of compromise (IoCs) across their environments.
- **Incident Response**: In the event of a breach, Falcon provides automated response capabilities, allowing organizations to contain and remediate threats quickly.
- **Real-World Impact**: The Falcon platform has proven effective in detecting sophisticated threats such as ransomware and advanced persistent threats (APTs). Its AI-driven approach allows organizations to stay ahead of evolving threats, significantly enhancing their incident response capabilities.

3. IBM Watson for Cyber Security

Overview: IBM Watson for Cyber Security is an AI-powered solution designed to augment security operations with advanced data analysis capabilities. By leveraging natural language processing (NLP) and machine learning, Watson helps security teams identify threats and respond effectively.

Key Features:

- **Threat Intelligence Analysis**: Watson analyzes vast amounts of unstructured data, including blogs, reports, and security advisories, to extract relevant threat intelligence. This enables organizations to stay informed about emerging threats and vulnerabilities.
- **Incident Response Automation**: The platform automates the investigation process by correlating incidents and providing recommendations for response actions based on historical data and context.
- **Collaboration with Security Analysts**: Watson enhances the capabilities of security analysts by providing insights and recommendations, enabling them to focus on higher-level strategic tasks rather than getting bogged down in repetitive analysis.
- **Real-World Impact**: Organizations that have adopted IBM Watson for Cyber Security report increased efficiency in threat detection and incident response. The system's ability to process and analyze large volumes of data enhances situational awareness and enables faster decision-making.

4. Palo Alto Networks: Cortex XDR

Overview: Palo Alto Networks offers Cortex XDR, an extended detection and response (XDR) platform that integrates AI and machine learning to provide comprehensive threat detection across endpoints, networks, and cloud environments.

Key Features:

- **Data Correlation**: Cortex XDR correlates data from various sources, including endpoint telemetry, network traffic, and cloud services, to identify threats that may span multiple attack vectors.
- **AI-Powered Threat Detection**: The platform utilizes advanced machine learning algorithms to analyze patterns and detect anomalies indicative of potential threats.
- **Automated Response**: Cortex XDR automates response actions based on predefined policies, enabling rapid containment of threats and reducing the burden on security teams.
- **Real-World Impact**: Organizations utilizing Cortex XDR have reported improved threat detection capabilities and reduced response times. The integrated approach allows for a more holistic view of the security landscape, making it easier to identify and address threats.

5. Microsoft Azure Sentinel

Overview: Microsoft Azure Sentinel is a cloud-native Security Information and Event Management (SIEM) solution that employs AI and machine learning to provide intelligent security analytics and threat intelligence across enterprise environments.

Key Features:

- **Smart Detection**: Sentinel uses machine learning models to analyze large volumes of security data, identifying potential threats and anomalies in real time.
- **Investigation and Response**: The platform offers automated investigation capabilities, enabling security teams to quickly assess incidents and respond effectively.
- **Integration with Microsoft Ecosystem**: Azure Sentinel integrates seamlessly with various Microsoft products and services, allowing for enhanced visibility and threat detection across Microsoft environments.
- **Real-World Impact**: Organizations that implement Azure Sentinel benefit from its ability to scale with their needs and provide comprehensive security analytics. The AI-driven insights help security teams prioritize threats and allocate resources more effectively.

6. FireEye: Helix Platform

Overview: FireEye's Helix platform combines security orchestration, automation, and response (SOAR) capabilities with advanced threat intelligence and analytics. It utilizes AI to enhance incident response workflows and improve security operations.

Key Features:

- **Threat Detection and Analysis**: Helix integrates data from various security tools and uses AI algorithms to detect threats and analyze incidents in real time.
- **Automated Playbooks**: The platform provides customizable playbooks that automate incident response processes, ensuring consistent and efficient handling of security events.
- **Collaboration and Communication**: Helix enhances collaboration among security teams by centralizing incident data and facilitating communication during investigations.
- **Real-World Impact**: FireEye Helix has proven valuable for organizations seeking to streamline their security operations. By automating incident response processes and providing actionable intelligence, Helix helps security teams respond to threats more effectively and efficiently.

These real-world examples illustrate the transformative impact of AI-enhanced cyber defense systems across various industries. By leveraging machine learning, natural language processing, and advanced data analytics, organizations can significantly improve their ability to detect, respond to, and mitigate cyber threats. As cyber adversaries continue to evolve, the integration of AI technologies will be essential for maintaining robust cybersecurity defenses and protecting sensitive data and assets. The continuous advancement of AI in cybersecurity not only enhances threat detection capabilities but also empowers security teams to respond to incidents more effectively, ensuring a proactive defense posture in an increasingly complex cyber landscape.

Chapter 3: Real-Time Threat Detection with AI

In the fast-paced world of cybersecurity, speed is critical. This chapter focuses on how artificial intelligence enables real-time threat detection, empowering systems to identify and respond to cyberattacks as they happen. We explore how AI leverages techniques like anomaly detection to spot irregular patterns in network traffic and behavioral analytics to monitor user and system activities for signs of compromise. Additionally, we look at the role of AI-powered monitoring tools that not only detect threats faster but also reduce false positives, allowing cybersecurity teams to focus on real dangers. This chapter reveals how AI is transforming the speed and accuracy of threat detection, making it a cornerstone of modern digital defense.

3.1 Anomaly Detection: Identifying Outliers in Network Traffic

Anomaly detection is a critical component of cybersecurity that focuses on identifying patterns in network traffic that deviate from established norms. This section delves into the concept of anomaly detection, its importance in network security, the methods employed for detecting anomalies, and real-world applications that demonstrate its effectiveness in protecting against cyber threats.

Understanding Anomaly Detection

Anomaly detection refers to the process of identifying unexpected or rare events in data that differ significantly from the majority of the dataset. In the context of network traffic, anomalies may indicate potential security incidents, such as intrusions, malware infections, or data exfiltration attempts. The primary objective of anomaly detection is to identify these outliers before they can lead to significant security breaches.

Importance in Network Security

The significance of anomaly detection in network security lies in its proactive approach to threat detection. Traditional security measures, such as signature-based detection, often rely on known attack patterns and may fail to identify novel or sophisticated threats. Anomaly detection complements these measures by:

Identifying Unknown Threats: Anomaly detection systems can identify previously unseen threats by recognizing deviations from normal behavior, allowing organizations to respond to emerging threats more effectively.

Reducing False Positives: By establishing a baseline of normal network behavior, anomaly detection can help differentiate between legitimate fluctuations in traffic and actual security incidents, reducing the number of false positives associated with traditional detection methods.

Enhancing Situational Awareness: Continuous monitoring of network traffic and the identification of anomalies provide security teams with valuable insights into the security posture of the organization, allowing for more informed decision-making.

Methods for Anomaly Detection in Network Traffic

Various methods can be employed for anomaly detection in network traffic, each with its strengths and limitations. These methods typically fall into three main categories: statistical techniques, machine learning algorithms, and deep learning approaches.

Statistical Techniques

Threshold-Based Methods: These methods define fixed thresholds for network metrics (e.g., bandwidth usage, packet rates) and flag any values exceeding these thresholds as anomalies. While simple and easy to implement, this approach may struggle with dynamic network environments where normal behavior can vary significantly over time.

Time-Series Analysis: Time-series models analyze historical data to identify trends and seasonal patterns. By modeling normal traffic patterns, deviations can be detected when observed traffic significantly diverges from the expected model. Techniques such as ARIMA (AutoRegressive Integrated Moving Average) and Seasonal Decomposition of Time Series (STL) can be employed in this context.

Machine Learning Algorithms

Clustering Algorithms: Algorithms like K-Means or DBSCAN can group similar data points based on their features. Any point that does not belong to any cluster can be considered an anomaly. For example, in network traffic, unusual connection attempts or data transfers may be flagged as anomalies when they do not fit into established usage patterns.

Supervised Learning: Supervised machine learning algorithms, such as decision trees, support vector machines (SVM), or random forests, can be trained on labeled datasets to identify normal and abnormal traffic patterns. Once trained, these models can classify incoming traffic in real-time.

Deep Learning Approaches

Autoencoders: Autoencoders are neural networks designed for unsupervised learning, often used in anomaly detection. They work by encoding input data into a lower-dimensional space and then reconstructing it back to the original space. Anomalies can be detected by measuring the reconstruction error; significant errors suggest that the input data does not conform to normal patterns.

Recurrent Neural Networks (RNNs): RNNs, especially Long Short-Term Memory (LSTM) networks, are well-suited for sequence prediction tasks and can analyze temporal patterns in network traffic. They can learn to model the normal behavior of network traffic over time, flagging deviations as anomalies.

Real-World Applications of Anomaly Detection

Intrusion Detection Systems (IDS)

Anomaly detection plays a pivotal role in modern Intrusion Detection Systems. By continuously monitoring network traffic and identifying deviations from established patterns, IDS can alert security teams to potential intrusion attempts. For example, if an employee's device begins sending an unusually high volume of data to an external server during off-hours, the IDS may flag this activity for further investigation.

Fraud Detection in Financial Transactions

Financial institutions leverage anomaly detection to monitor transaction patterns and identify fraudulent activities. For instance, if a customer's credit card is suddenly used for large purchases in a different country within a short time frame, the anomaly detection system may flag this transaction for review, reducing the risk of fraud.

Monitoring Internet of Things (IoT) Devices

The proliferation of IoT devices has introduced new vulnerabilities and attack vectors. Anomaly detection can help secure these devices by monitoring their network behavior. For example, if an IoT camera begins transmitting data at an unusual rate or communicating with unauthorized IP addresses, the anomaly detection system can trigger alerts to the security team.

Cloud Security Monitoring

Cloud environments are dynamic and often involve multiple users accessing shared resources. Anomaly detection can help identify unauthorized access attempts, unusual resource usage patterns, or data exfiltration activities. For example, if a cloud storage account experiences a sudden surge in data downloads from an unfamiliar IP address, the anomaly detection system can flag this behavior as suspicious.

Challenges in Anomaly Detection

While anomaly detection is a powerful tool in cybersecurity, it is not without its challenges:

Dynamic Environments: Network traffic patterns can change over time due to legitimate business activities, making it difficult to establish accurate baselines for normal behavior.

High Volume of Data: The sheer volume of network traffic can overwhelm traditional anomaly detection systems, leading to slow response times or missed anomalies.

Evolving Threat Landscape: Cyber threats continue to evolve, with attackers employing advanced techniques to evade detection. Anomaly detection systems must continually adapt to new attack methods.

False Positives: While anomaly detection aims to reduce false positives, it is still a challenge. Security teams may become desensitized to alerts if they receive too many false positives, leading to potential oversight of genuine threats.

Anomaly detection is a vital technique in identifying outliers in network traffic, providing organizations with a proactive approach to cybersecurity. By leveraging statistical methods, machine learning algorithms, and deep learning techniques, organizations can enhance their ability to detect and respond to potential threats in real-time. As cyber threats become more sophisticated, the integration of anomaly detection systems into cybersecurity frameworks will be essential for safeguarding sensitive data and maintaining a robust security posture. The continuous evolution of these systems will ensure that organizations remain equipped to combat emerging threats effectively.

3.2 Behavioral Analytics: AI's Role in Identifying User and Entity Behavior

Behavioral analytics is an increasingly vital component of cybersecurity that focuses on understanding and monitoring the behavior of users and entities within an organization's network. By leveraging artificial intelligence (AI) and machine learning, behavioral analytics tools can identify abnormal activities that may indicate potential security threats, such as insider threats, account takeovers, or data breaches. This section explores the role of AI in behavioral analytics, the techniques used for analysis, its applications in cybersecurity, and the challenges associated with implementing these solutions.

Understanding Behavioral Analytics

Behavioral analytics involves the collection and analysis of data regarding user and entity interactions within an IT environment. It aims to establish a baseline of normal behavior for users, devices, and applications. By continuously monitoring and analyzing this behavior, organizations can detect deviations that may signify security incidents.

Key aspects of behavioral analytics include:

User Behavior: Understanding how individual users interact with systems, applications, and data, including login times, access patterns, and file usage.

Entity Behavior: Analyzing the behavior of entities such as devices, applications, and services within the network to identify irregularities that could indicate compromised assets.

Contextual Awareness: Considering the context of behavior, including location, time, and environmental factors, to differentiate between legitimate and suspicious activities.

The Role of AI in Behavioral Analytics

AI and machine learning play a transformative role in enhancing the capabilities of behavioral analytics. These technologies enable organizations to process vast amounts of data, identify patterns, and make data-driven decisions in real-time. Key contributions of AI in this context include:

Automated Baseline Creation: AI algorithms can automatically establish a baseline of normal behavior for users and entities based on historical data. This baseline serves as a reference point for detecting anomalies.

Real-Time Monitoring: AI-driven systems continuously monitor user and entity behavior, allowing for immediate detection of unusual activities that deviate from established norms.

Contextual Analysis: AI can analyze contextual factors to provide deeper insights into user behavior. For example, if a user accesses sensitive data from an unusual location or at an atypical time, the system can flag this activity for further investigation.

Adaptive Learning: Machine learning models can learn and adapt to changes in user behavior over time. This means that as users evolve their patterns of interaction, the system can adjust its baseline accordingly, minimizing false positives.

Techniques Used in Behavioral Analytics

Several techniques are employed in behavioral analytics to analyze user and entity behavior effectively:

Statistical Analysis

Statistical methods involve using historical data to define normal behavior patterns. Algorithms calculate metrics such as mean, standard deviation, and percentile thresholds to establish what constitutes typical behavior.

For instance, if a user typically logs into their account during business hours, any login attempts during unusual hours may be flagged as potential anomalies.

Machine Learning Algorithms

Clustering: Algorithms like K-Means or DBSCAN can group similar behaviors to identify clusters of normal activity. Any behavior that falls outside these clusters can be marked as suspicious.

Classification: Supervised learning algorithms can be trained on labeled datasets to distinguish between normal and abnormal behaviors. Techniques like decision trees, random forests, and support vector machines can be applied in this context.

Deep Learning

Neural networks can model complex patterns in user and entity behavior. Techniques like recurrent neural networks (RNNs) or long short-term memory (LSTM) networks are particularly useful for analyzing sequential data, such as user login patterns over time.

Behavioral Scoring

Behavioral scoring systems assign risk scores to user actions based on their deviation from normal behavior. For example, accessing sensitive files from an unrecognized device or location may result in a higher risk score, prompting further investigation. Applications of Behavioral Analytics in Cybersecurity

Insider Threat Detection

Behavioral analytics can be instrumental in detecting insider threats, where employees intentionally or unintentionally compromise security. By monitoring user behavior for signs of unusual activity, organizations can identify potential insider threats before they escalate. For example, if an employee downloads an unusually high volume of sensitive data or accesses restricted areas of the network without prior authorization, these behaviors can trigger alerts for security teams.

Account Takeover Prevention

Account takeovers occur when unauthorized individuals gain access to user accounts, often through phishing attacks or credential theft. Behavioral analytics can help identify account takeovers by monitoring for irregular login patterns. If a user typically logs in from one geographic location and suddenly attempts to access their account from a different country, the system can flag this as a potential takeover attempt.

Data Loss Prevention (DLP)

Behavioral analytics can enhance data loss prevention strategies by monitoring user actions related to sensitive data. By analyzing how users interact with files, organizations can identify suspicious activities, such as copying large amounts of data to external drives or emailing sensitive information to unverified recipients. This enables security teams to take immediate action to prevent data breaches.

Cloud Security Monitoring

With the increasing adoption of cloud services, behavioral analytics has become crucial for monitoring user interactions in cloud environments. By analyzing user behavior across various cloud applications, organizations can detect unauthorized access attempts, abnormal file sharing activities, or data exfiltration efforts.

Challenges in Implementing Behavioral Analytics

While behavioral analytics offers significant benefits, several challenges must be addressed for effective implementation:

Data Privacy Concerns

Monitoring user behavior raises data privacy concerns, as organizations must balance security needs with users' rights to privacy. It is essential to ensure that behavioral analytics comply with regulations such as GDPR and CCPA and that data collection practices are transparent.

False Positives

Despite advancements in AI and machine learning, behavioral analytics can still generate false positives, where legitimate activities are incorrectly flagged as suspicious. This can lead to alert fatigue among security teams and may result in critical threats being overlooked.

Dynamic Work Environments

The modern workforce often operates in dynamic environments, such as remote work or flexible schedules. Behavioral analytics must adapt to these changes, continuously updating baselines to reflect evolving user behaviors and roles.

Integration with Existing Security Tools

For behavioral analytics to be effective, it must integrate seamlessly with existing security infrastructure, such as Security Information and Event Management (SIEM) systems, Intrusion Detection Systems (IDS), and endpoint protection tools. This integration can be complex and requires careful planning.

Behavioral analytics, powered by AI and machine learning, is a critical tool in identifying user and entity behavior patterns that may indicate security threats. By establishing baselines of normal behavior and continuously monitoring for anomalies, organizations can proactively detect and respond to potential threats. Applications in insider threat detection, account takeover prevention, data loss prevention, and cloud security monitoring demonstrate the effectiveness of behavioral analytics in enhancing cybersecurity.

Despite challenges such as data privacy concerns and the risk of false positives, the benefits of implementing behavioral analytics far outweigh the drawbacks. As cyber threats continue to evolve, the role of AI in behavioral analytics will be paramount in helping organizations stay ahead of potential security incidents and maintain a robust security posture.

3.3 AI-Powered Monitoring Tools: Real-Time Threat Detection and Alerts

In an increasingly complex cybersecurity landscape, traditional monitoring methods often struggle to keep pace with the rapid evolution of threats. Cyberattacks are becoming more sophisticated, leveraging advanced techniques that can evade conventional detection systems. To address these challenges, organizations are increasingly turning to AI-powered monitoring tools that offer real-time threat detection and alerting capabilities. This section explores the features and advantages of these tools, their underlying technologies, and their applications in cybersecurity.

Understanding AI-Powered Monitoring Tools

AI-powered monitoring tools are advanced systems designed to analyze vast amounts of data from various sources in real time to identify potential security threats. These tools use artificial intelligence and machine learning algorithms to automate threat detection, enabling organizations to respond to incidents more swiftly and effectively. Key features of these tools include:

Real-Time Data Processing: AI monitoring tools continuously collect and analyze data from network traffic, user behavior, endpoints, and other security telemetry, allowing for immediate identification of potential threats.

Anomaly Detection: By establishing a baseline of normal behavior, AI algorithms can detect deviations that may indicate malicious activity. For example, if a user suddenly accesses sensitive data outside of their normal work hours, the system can flag this as a potential security incident.

Automated Alerts: When a threat is detected, these tools can generate automated alerts to notify security teams, enabling a swift response. Alerts can include detailed information about the threat, such as its nature, affected systems, and recommended response actions.

Integration with Existing Security Infrastructure: AI-powered monitoring tools can integrate with other security systems, such as Security Information and Event Management (SIEM) solutions and Intrusion Detection Systems (IDS), to provide a more comprehensive view of the organization's security posture.

Technologies Behind AI-Powered Monitoring Tools

The effectiveness of AI-powered monitoring tools is largely attributable to several key technologies:

Machine Learning Algorithms

Supervised Learning: These algorithms are trained on labeled datasets to recognize patterns associated with normal and abnormal behavior. Once trained, they can classify new data points in real time, identifying potential threats based on historical data.

Unsupervised Learning: In contrast, unsupervised learning algorithms analyze unlabeled data to discover hidden patterns. This is particularly useful for detecting novel threats, as the system does not rely on predefined categories.

Natural Language Processing (NLP)

NLP techniques enable AI-powered tools to analyze unstructured data, such as logs, emails, and security reports, extracting valuable insights and identifying indicators of compromise (IoCs). For example, NLP can be used to scan threat intelligence reports for emerging threats that may not yet be included in signature-based detection systems.

Behavioral Analysis

AI monitoring tools leverage behavioral analysis to establish baselines of normal activity for users and systems. By continuously monitoring deviations from these baselines, the tools can quickly identify suspicious behavior and generate alerts.

Big Data Analytics

The ability to process and analyze large volumes of data is crucial for effective threat detection. AI-powered monitoring tools utilize big data technologies to ingest, store, and analyze security data from various sources, allowing for comprehensive visibility across the network.

Applications of AI-Powered Monitoring Tools in Cybersecurity

Intrusion Detection and Prevention

AI-powered monitoring tools play a vital role in intrusion detection and prevention systems (IDPS). By analyzing network traffic and user behavior in real time, these tools can identify suspicious activities, such as unauthorized access attempts or lateral movement within the network. When a potential intrusion is detected, the system can automatically block the malicious activity and alert the security team.

Endpoint Protection

AI monitoring tools can enhance endpoint protection by continuously monitoring device activity for signs of compromise. For example, if a workstation exhibits unusual behavior, such as executing unfamiliar processes or communicating with known malicious IP addresses, the monitoring tool can flag this behavior for further investigation.

Cloud Security Monitoring

With the increasing adoption of cloud services, AI-powered monitoring tools are essential for securing cloud environments. These tools can monitor user access patterns, API usage, and data transfers within cloud applications, identifying anomalies that may indicate unauthorized access or data exfiltration attempts.

Threat Intelligence Integration

AI monitoring tools can integrate with threat intelligence feeds to stay updated on the latest vulnerabilities and attack vectors. By analyzing this intelligence alongside real-time data, organizations can proactively identify potential threats and adjust their security measures accordingly.

Incident Response Automation

AI-powered monitoring tools can automate incident response processes by generating playbooks that outline specific actions to take when a threat is detected. This can include isolating affected systems, blocking malicious IP addresses, and notifying security personnel. By automating these tasks, organizations can reduce response times and minimize potential damage from cyber incidents.

Benefits of AI-Powered Monitoring Tools

Enhanced Threat Detection Capabilities

The combination of AI and machine learning allows monitoring tools to detect a wider range of threats, including zero-day vulnerabilities and advanced persistent threats (APTs) that may bypass traditional detection methods.

Reduced Response Times

Automated alerts and incident response capabilities enable security teams to act quickly in the event of a detected threat. This rapid response is critical in mitigating the potential impact of a cyber attack.

Improved Accuracy and Efficiency

By leveraging AI to analyze data, organizations can reduce the number of false positives generated by traditional monitoring methods. This allows security teams to focus on genuine threats and streamline their incident response efforts.

Scalability

AI-powered monitoring tools can easily scale to accommodate growing amounts of data as organizations expand their networks and user bases. This scalability is essential in today's fast-paced digital landscape.

Proactive Security Posture

Continuous monitoring and real-time threat detection empower organizations to adopt a proactive security posture. By identifying and addressing potential threats before they escalate, organizations can minimize the risk of data breaches and other security incidents.

Challenges and Considerations

While AI-powered monitoring tools offer significant advantages, organizations must also consider the following challenges:

Data Privacy and Compliance

Monitoring user behavior and network traffic raises data privacy concerns. Organizations must ensure that their monitoring practices comply with regulations such as GDPR and CCPA and that users are informed about data collection practices.

Integration Complexity

Integrating AI-powered monitoring tools with existing security infrastructure can be complex and may require significant resources. Organizations should carefully plan the integration process to ensure seamless operation and data sharing.

Dependence on Quality Data

The effectiveness of AI-powered monitoring tools relies heavily on the quality of the data being analyzed. Incomplete or inaccurate data can lead to poor detection performance and increased false positives.

Evolving Threat Landscape

As cyber threats continue to evolve, monitoring tools must also adapt. Organizations should invest in ongoing updates and improvements to their AI algorithms to ensure that they remain effective against emerging threats.

AI-powered monitoring tools have become indispensable in the realm of cybersecurity, offering real-time threat detection and alerting capabilities that significantly enhance an organization's security posture. By leveraging machine learning, behavioral analysis, and big data analytics, these tools provide comprehensive visibility into network activities and user behaviors, enabling organizations to swiftly identify and respond to potential threats.

As cyber threats become increasingly sophisticated, the importance of adopting AI-driven monitoring solutions will continue to grow. While challenges such as data privacy and integration complexity exist, the benefits of enhanced threat detection, reduced response times, and a proactive security posture make AI-powered monitoring tools a critical investment for organizations seeking to safeguard their digital assets. In an era where cyber resilience is paramount, these tools will play a vital role in helping organizations navigate the complexities of modern cybersecurity.

Chapter 4: AI-Driven Incident Response and Mitigation

In this chapter, we delve into the transformative impact of artificial intelligence on incident response and mitigation strategies in cybersecurity. As cyber threats become increasingly sophisticated, the need for rapid and effective responses is paramount. We explore how AI automates critical aspects of incident response, enabling organizations to react to security incidents more swiftly and efficiently than ever before. Through the use of machine learning algorithms and intelligent automation, AI can analyze incidents, prioritize responses, and even initiate mitigation actions without human intervention. Additionally, we discuss the importance of AI in forensic analysis, helping security teams uncover the root causes of breaches and refine their defenses. By integrating AI into their incident response frameworks, organizations can significantly enhance their resilience against cyber threats, turning potential crises into opportunities for improvement and strengthening their overall security posture.

4.1 Autonomous Incident Response: How AI Accelerates Reaction Time

In the rapidly evolving landscape of cybersecurity, organizations face an increasing number of sophisticated threats that can emerge without warning. As cyberattacks become more complex and damaging, the need for effective and timely incident response has never been greater. Traditional incident response methods often struggle to keep pace, as they rely heavily on manual processes and human intervention, leading to delays that can result in significant data breaches and financial losses. To address these challenges, organizations are turning to AI-driven autonomous incident response solutions, which can dramatically accelerate reaction times and enhance overall security posture. This section explores how AI facilitates autonomous incident response, the benefits it offers, and the challenges organizations may face in its implementation.

Understanding Autonomous Incident Response

Autonomous incident response refers to the use of artificial intelligence and machine learning technologies to automate the identification, assessment, and response to security incidents without significant human intervention. By leveraging advanced algorithms, AI-driven systems can analyze vast amounts of data, identify threats in real-time, and take pre-defined actions to mitigate potential damage. The core components of autonomous incident response include:

Automated Threat Detection: AI algorithms continuously monitor network activity, user behavior, and system logs to identify signs of security incidents. By using machine learning models trained on historical attack data, these systems can distinguish between normal and anomalous behavior, allowing them to detect potential threats as they arise.

Real-Time Analysis: AI-driven tools can analyze data in real-time, providing security teams with immediate insights into the nature and severity of an incident. This capability is crucial for understanding the context of a threat and determining the appropriate response.

Automated Response Actions: Once a threat is detected, autonomous incident response systems can execute pre-defined response actions based on the type and severity of the incident. This can include isolating affected systems, blocking malicious IP addresses, terminating compromised user sessions, or implementing network segmentation.

Post-Incident Analysis: After an incident has been addressed, AI systems can conduct post-incident analysis to evaluate the response's effectiveness. This analysis helps organizations refine their response strategies and improve their overall security posture.

The Role of AI in Accelerating Reaction Time

AI accelerates reaction times in incident response through several key mechanisms:

Speed and Efficiency of Threat Detection

Traditional security monitoring solutions often rely on signature-based detection methods that can be slow to identify new or evolving threats. In contrast, AI algorithms can analyze vast amounts of data from various sources at high speed, allowing for rapid identification of anomalies that may indicate an incident. For example, if a network experiences an unexpected surge in outbound traffic, an AI-powered monitoring tool can quickly flag this behavior and initiate a response.

Reduced Mean Time to Detect (MTTD)

The mean time to detect (MTTD) is a critical metric in incident response that measures the time taken to identify a security incident. By leveraging AI, organizations can significantly reduce MTTD, enabling security teams to respond to threats before they escalate into serious breaches. AI's ability to analyze data continuously and in real-time ensures that potential incidents are detected swiftly, allowing for immediate action.

Automated Triage and Prioritization

Upon detecting a potential incident, AI-driven systems can automatically triage alerts based on the severity of the threat and its potential impact on the organization. This prioritization allows security teams to focus their efforts on the most critical incidents first, improving overall response efficiency. For example, a ransomware attack may be flagged as high priority, prompting immediate investigation, while less severe threats can be queued for later review.

Decision-Making Support

AI can assist security teams in making informed decisions during an incident response. By providing relevant context, historical data, and recommendations based on past incidents, AI systems can enhance human decision-making processes. This support can be invaluable in high-pressure situations where swift, accurate decisions are essential.

Learning and Adaptation

Machine learning algorithms improve over time as they are exposed to new data. Autonomous incident response systems can learn from previous incidents, refining their detection and response capabilities to adapt to the evolving threat landscape. This continuous learning process ensures that AI-driven systems remain effective against new and emerging threats, further accelerating reaction times.

Benefits of Autonomous Incident Response

Faster Response Times

One of the most significant benefits of autonomous incident response is the reduction in response times. By automating threat detection and response actions, organizations can address incidents almost instantaneously, minimizing the potential damage and disruption caused by cyberattacks.

Increased Efficiency

By automating routine tasks, security teams can focus on more complex and strategic aspects of incident response. This increased efficiency not only enhances the effectiveness of the security team but also allows organizations to allocate their resources more effectively.

Improved Incident Management

Autonomous incident response systems can streamline the incident management process, providing comprehensive visibility into ongoing incidents and their status. This improved visibility allows security teams to manage incidents more effectively and ensures that all relevant stakeholders are informed of the situation.

Consistent and Reliable Responses

AI-driven systems follow pre-defined protocols for incident response, ensuring that responses are consistent and reliable. This consistency reduces the risk of human error, which can occur in high-pressure situations when security teams are responding to incidents manually.

Cost Savings

By reducing the time and resources required for incident response, organizations can achieve significant cost savings. Faster detection and resolution of incidents also help prevent costly data breaches and reputational damage.

Challenges in Implementing Autonomous Incident Response

Despite the numerous benefits, organizations may face several challenges in implementing autonomous incident response systems:

Complexity of Implementation

Deploying AI-driven solutions requires a careful understanding of the organization's existing infrastructure and security protocols. The integration of autonomous incident response systems with existing tools and processes can be complex and may require substantial investment.

Data Quality and Availability

The effectiveness of AI-powered systems relies on the quality and availability of data. Organizations must ensure that their data is accurate, complete, and up-to-date to enable effective threat detection and response.

Overreliance on Automation

While autonomous incident response systems can enhance efficiency, there is a risk that organizations may become over-reliant on automation. Human oversight is still essential in certain situations, particularly in complex incidents where nuanced decision-making is required.

Privacy and Compliance Concerns

The automation of incident response processes may raise privacy and compliance concerns. Organizations must ensure that their automated responses do not inadvertently violate data protection regulations or compromise user privacy.

Adapting to Evolving Threats

The threat landscape is continually changing, and organizations must ensure that their autonomous incident response systems are adaptable to emerging threats. Continuous updates and learning mechanisms are essential to maintain the effectiveness of these systems.

Autonomous incident response powered by AI represents a transformative approach to cybersecurity, enabling organizations to accelerate reaction times and enhance their ability to respond to threats in real-time. By automating threat detection, analysis, and response actions, AI-driven systems can significantly reduce mean time to detect and mitigate potential incidents before they escalate.

While challenges such as implementation complexity and data quality exist, the benefits of faster response times, increased efficiency, and improved incident management make autonomous incident response an essential component of a modern cybersecurity strategy. As organizations continue to navigate the complexities of the digital landscape, leveraging AI to enhance incident response capabilities will be critical in safeguarding their assets and maintaining resilience against evolving cyber threats.

4.2 AI-Assisted Forensics: Uncovering the Source of Cyberattacks

In the wake of a cyberattack, understanding the source and nature of the intrusion is crucial for both mitigating immediate damage and preventing future incidents. Traditional forensic techniques often involve extensive manual analysis of logs, network traffic, and system artifacts, which can be time-consuming and resource-intensive. As cyber threats evolve and become increasingly sophisticated, the need for advanced tools and methodologies to aid in forensic investigations has become paramount. AI-assisted forensics is emerging as a transformative approach that leverages artificial intelligence and machine learning to streamline and enhance the investigation process. This section delves into how AI aids forensic investigations, the technologies involved, its benefits, and the challenges organizations may face when implementing these solutions.

Understanding AI-Assisted Forensics

AI-assisted forensics refers to the application of artificial intelligence and machine learning techniques to automate and improve the processes involved in digital forensic investigations. This includes the identification, collection, analysis, and reporting of evidence related to cyber incidents. The core components of AI-assisted forensics include:

Data Collection: Gathering data from various sources, such as network logs, endpoint devices, cloud services, and other digital footprints left by cybercriminals. AI can automate the collection process, ensuring comprehensive data capture while minimizing human error.

Data Analysis: Utilizing AI algorithms to analyze vast amounts of collected data for patterns, anomalies, and indicators of compromise (IoCs). This analysis can reveal critical insights about the attack, including its source, method of execution, and potential targets.

Evidence Correlation: AI can correlate evidence from disparate sources, identifying connections and relationships between different data points. This correlation helps investigators piece together the timeline and context of an attack.

Reporting and Visualization: AI-assisted tools can automatically generate reports and visualizations that summarize findings and provide insights into the attack's nature and impact. This can include timelines of events, affected systems, and recommendations for remediation.

How AI Enhances Forensic Investigations

AI enhances forensic investigations in several ways:

Speed and Efficiency of Data Processing

The sheer volume of data generated during a cyber incident can be overwhelming for human investigators. AI algorithms can process and analyze this data at incredible speeds, significantly reducing the time required to identify key evidence. For example, while a human analyst may take days to sift through logs, AI can quickly analyze them, identifying patterns or anomalies that may indicate malicious activity.

Automated Threat Detection

AI-assisted forensic tools can utilize machine learning models to detect known and unknown threats in real-time. By training models on historical attack data, these tools can identify patterns indicative of specific attack vectors, such as malware infections, phishing attempts, or insider threats. This automated detection capability enhances the investigator's ability to respond promptly to threats.

Anomaly Detection and Behavioral Analysis

AI can establish baselines of normal behavior for users and systems, allowing it to identify deviations that may indicate an attack. For example, if a user account suddenly attempts to access sensitive files it typically does not interact with, this behavior can be flagged as suspicious. By focusing on behavioral anomalies, AI-assisted forensics can uncover stealthy attacks that traditional methods might miss.

Predictive Analytics

By analyzing historical data and identifying patterns, AI can also aid in predicting potential future attacks. This predictive capability allows organizations to proactively strengthen their defenses and prepare for potential threats.

Enhanced Visualization Tools

AI-assisted forensics often includes advanced visualization capabilities that can present complex data in an easily digestible format. Interactive dashboards, heat maps, and timelines help investigators quickly grasp the context of an attack, making it easier to communicate findings to stakeholders.

Benefits of AI-Assisted Forensics

Faster Incident Recovery

The speed of AI-assisted forensic investigations leads to faster identification of the source and nature of cyberattacks, allowing organizations to implement recovery measures sooner. Quick recovery minimizes downtime and reduces the overall impact of an incident.

Improved Accuracy in Investigations

AI can enhance the accuracy of forensic investigations by reducing the likelihood of human error in data analysis. Automated processes help ensure that critical evidence is not overlooked, leading to more reliable conclusions about the attack.

Cost-Effectiveness

By streamlining the forensic process, AI can reduce the time and resources needed for investigations. This cost-effectiveness is especially beneficial for organizations that may not have the resources to conduct extensive manual forensic analyses.

Enhanced Decision-Making

AI-assisted forensics provides investigators with actionable insights and recommendations based on data analysis. This information can guide decision-making, helping organizations take the necessary steps to prevent future incidents.

Comprehensive Threat Intelligence

AI can aggregate data from various sources, providing a holistic view of the threat landscape. This comprehensive threat intelligence is valuable not only for forensic investigations but also for enhancing overall cybersecurity posture.

Challenges in Implementing AI-Assisted Forensics

Despite its advantages, organizations may encounter several challenges when implementing AI-assisted forensic solutions:

Complexity of Integration

Integrating AI-assisted forensics with existing security infrastructure and tools can be complex and may require significant investment in time and resources. Organizations must ensure compatibility and seamless data flow between systems.

Data Privacy and Compliance Issues

The collection and analysis of data during forensic investigations may raise privacy and compliance concerns. Organizations must navigate regulations such as GDPR and HIPAA to ensure that their forensic practices comply with legal requirements.

Quality of Data

The effectiveness of AI-assisted forensics depends on the quality and completeness of the data being analyzed. Inaccurate or incomplete data can lead to misleading conclusions, emphasizing the need for robust data management practices.

Need for Skilled Personnel

While AI can automate many processes, skilled personnel are still required to oversee investigations and interpret findings. Organizations must invest in training and retaining skilled forensic analysts to maximize the benefits of AI technologies.

Evolving Threat Landscape

Cyber threats are continually evolving, requiring AI-assisted forensic tools to adapt to new tactics and techniques used by attackers. Organizations must ensure that their AI systems are regularly updated and trained on the latest threat intelligence.

AI-assisted forensics is revolutionizing the way organizations investigate and respond to cyberattacks. By automating data collection, analysis, and reporting, AI tools enhance the speed, accuracy, and efficiency of forensic investigations, allowing organizations to uncover the source and nature of incidents more effectively. With the ability to detect anomalies, correlate evidence, and provide actionable insights, AI-assisted forensics empowers organizations to respond to threats proactively and reduce the overall impact of cyber incidents.

While challenges such as integration complexity, data privacy concerns, and the need for skilled personnel exist, the benefits of implementing AI-assisted forensic solutions far outweigh the drawbacks. As cyber threats continue to evolve, embracing AI technologies in forensic investigations will be crucial for organizations seeking to bolster their cybersecurity defenses and maintain resilience in an increasingly hostile digital landscape. By leveraging AI-assisted forensics, organizations can not only uncover the source of cyberattacks but also fortify their defenses against future threats.

4.3 Reducing Human Error: How AI Can Optimize Cybersecurity Workflows

Human error remains one of the most significant vulnerabilities in cybersecurity. Despite the advancements in technology, research consistently shows that a large percentage of security breaches are attributed to mistakes made by employees, ranging from misconfigured systems to falling victim to phishing attacks. As organizations increasingly recognize the critical need for robust cybersecurity measures, there is a growing consensus that integrating artificial intelligence (AI) into cybersecurity workflows can play a pivotal role in minimizing human error. This section explores how AI optimizes cybersecurity processes, reduces the likelihood of human mistakes, and ultimately strengthens an organization's defense against cyber threats.

Understanding the Impact of Human Error on Cybersecurity

Human error can manifest in various ways within an organization's cybersecurity practices, including:

Misconfiguration of Security Tools: Employees tasked with managing security tools may inadvertently misconfigure settings, leaving systems vulnerable to attacks. For example, an incorrectly set firewall rule could allow unauthorized access to sensitive data.

Phishing and Social Engineering Attacks: Despite training programs, employees may still fall victim to phishing emails or social engineering tactics, leading to credential theft or malware infections. The human element in these attacks is often exploited by cybercriminals, making education and vigilance essential.

Inconsistent Application of Security Protocols: Variability in how employees adhere to security protocols can create gaps in an organization's defenses. For instance, one team may follow password policies diligently while another may neglect to update passwords regularly.

Delayed Response to Threats: Security teams may face information overload due to the sheer volume of alerts generated by security systems. In such situations, human analysts may overlook critical alerts or take too long to respond, allowing threats to escalate.

How AI Can Optimize Cybersecurity Workflows

AI can significantly enhance cybersecurity workflows in several ways, addressing the root causes of human error and improving overall security posture:

Automating Routine Tasks

AI-driven automation can take over repetitive and time-consuming tasks that are prone to human error. For example, security incident response automation can manage alerts, perform initial triage, and escalate genuine threats to human analysts. This reduces the risk of oversight, allowing security teams to focus on higher-level analysis and decision-making.

Enhancing Threat Detection

AI-powered systems can analyze vast amounts of data in real-time, identifying patterns and anomalies that may indicate security incidents. By automating the detection of suspicious activity, AI helps minimize the chances of human oversight. For example, machine learning algorithms can be trained to recognize the typical behavior of users and flag any deviations, such as unusual login times or locations.

Providing Contextual Insights

AI can offer contextual insights that aid human analysts in understanding security incidents. By aggregating and correlating data from multiple sources, AI tools can provide a clearer picture of a potential threat. This contextual information helps analysts prioritize alerts and make informed decisions, reducing the likelihood of incorrect assessments.

Improving Security Training

AI can enhance security training programs by providing personalized and adaptive learning experiences. For example, AI algorithms can analyze employee behavior and tailor training content to address specific vulnerabilities or knowledge gaps. By offering targeted training, organizations can reduce the risk of human error in security practices.

Facilitating Incident Response

AI can streamline incident response processes by providing automated playbooks that guide analysts through the response steps based on predefined protocols. For instance, if a malware infection is detected, AI can suggest immediate actions such as isolating affected systems, terminating malicious processes, or deploying patches. This structured approach helps ensure that no critical steps are overlooked.

Augmenting Decision-Making

AI can assist security professionals in making more informed decisions during high-pressure situations. By analyzing historical incident data, AI can provide recommendations for response actions based on past successful outcomes. This augmented decision-making reduces the risk of impulsive or poorly thought-out actions that may arise from stress or urgency.

Monitoring Compliance and Policy Adherence

AI can continuously monitor employee behavior and system configurations to ensure compliance with established security policies. For example, AI tools can automatically flag non-compliant configurations or remind employees to update passwords, mitigating the risk of human error related to policy violations.

Benefits of AI-Optimized Cybersecurity Workflows

Reduced Risk of Security Breaches

By automating routine tasks, enhancing threat detection, and providing contextual insights, AI reduces the risk of human error that can lead to security breaches. Organizations that implement AI in their workflows are better positioned to detect and respond to threats swiftly.

Increased Operational Efficiency

Automating repetitive tasks frees up security professionals to focus on more complex and strategic aspects of cybersecurity. This increased efficiency allows organizations to allocate their resources more effectively and respond to threats more proactively.

Improved Employee Engagement and Training

AI-driven training programs enhance employee engagement by offering personalized learning experiences. As employees become more knowledgeable about security threats and best practices, their ability to recognize and respond to risks improves, further reducing human error.

Enhanced Incident Response Capabilities

Streamlined incident response processes ensure that organizations can respond to threats quickly and effectively. By providing automated playbooks and contextual insights, AI enhances the overall quality of incident response efforts.

Stronger Security Posture

The cumulative effect of reduced human error, increased efficiency, and improved training leads to a stronger overall security posture. Organizations that optimize their cybersecurity workflows with AI are better equipped to withstand evolving cyber threats.

Challenges in Implementing AI in Cybersecurity Workflows

Despite the numerous benefits of integrating AI into cybersecurity workflows, organizations may face several challenges:

Integration Complexity

Implementing AI solutions within existing security frameworks can be complex. Organizations must ensure that AI tools integrate seamlessly with their current systems and processes, which may require significant time and resources.

Data Quality and Availability

The effectiveness of AI algorithms depends on the quality and availability of data. Organizations must ensure that they have access to accurate, relevant, and up-to-date data to train AI models effectively.

Resistance to Change

Employees may be resistant to adopting new AI-driven processes, particularly if they perceive AI as a threat to their roles. Organizations must foster a culture of collaboration and emphasize that AI is a tool designed to enhance human capabilities rather than replace them.

Addressing Privacy and Compliance Concerns

The implementation of AI in cybersecurity workflows may raise privacy and compliance concerns, especially when dealing with sensitive data. Organizations must navigate regulations and ensure that their AI practices align with legal requirements.

Continuous Learning and Adaptation

The evolving nature of cyber threats necessitates that AI algorithms be continuously updated and refined. Organizations must invest in ongoing training and development to keep AI systems effective against new attack vectors.

AI has the potential to revolutionize cybersecurity workflows by significantly reducing human error and enhancing overall security posture. By automating routine tasks, improving threat detection, and providing contextual insights, AI enables organizations to mitigate the risks associated with human mistakes. The integration of AI into cybersecurity processes not only streamlines operations but also empowers security professionals to make informed decisions and respond to threats effectively.

While challenges such as integration complexity, data quality, and resistance to change exist, the benefits of optimizing cybersecurity workflows with AI far outweigh the drawbacks. As organizations continue to face increasingly sophisticated cyber threats, leveraging AI to reduce human error will be essential for maintaining robust cybersecurity defenses and ensuring a resilient response to emerging risks. By embracing AI technologies, organizations can enhance their security capabilities and create a more secure digital environment.

Chapter 5: Machine Learning in Threat Intelligence

In this chapter, we explore the critical role of machine learning in enhancing threat intelligence, an essential component of proactive cybersecurity strategies. Machine learning algorithms can sift through vast amounts of data from various sources—such as network logs, threat feeds, and historical incident data—to identify emerging patterns and anomalies that may indicate potential threats. We discuss how these predictive models allow organizations to anticipate and prepare for future attacks, rather than merely reacting to them. Furthermore, we examine the applications of machine learning in data mining and its ability to correlate disparate data points to generate actionable intelligence. By leveraging machine learning, organizations can develop a more nuanced understanding of the threat landscape, enabling them to respond more effectively to cyber risks and improve their overall security posture. This chapter highlights the transformative potential of machine learning in threat intelligence and underscores its necessity in the modern cybersecurity arsenal.

5.1 Data Mining for Cyber Threats: Using ML to Extract Insights

In the ever-evolving landscape of cybersecurity, organizations are inundated with vast amounts of data generated from various sources, including network logs, user activities, and system alerts. While this data holds valuable insights, extracting meaningful information to preemptively identify cyber threats has become a significant challenge. Traditional methods of data analysis often struggle to keep pace with the sheer volume and complexity of modern cyber threats. Machine learning (ML) has emerged as a powerful tool for data mining, enabling organizations to sift through massive datasets and uncover actionable insights to enhance their cybersecurity posture. This section explores how data mining through machine learning can help identify cyber threats, the methodologies involved, and its implications for organizations.

Understanding Data Mining in Cybersecurity

Data mining refers to the process of discovering patterns, correlations, and anomalies within large datasets to extract valuable insights. In the context of cybersecurity, data mining involves analyzing various data sources to identify signs of potential threats, vulnerabilities, and security incidents. The process typically includes several steps:

Data Collection: Gathering relevant data from diverse sources such as logs from firewalls, intrusion detection systems (IDS), antivirus software, and network traffic. This data can be structured (e.g., databases) or unstructured (e.g., text logs).

Data Preprocessing: Cleaning and preparing the collected data for analysis. This involves removing irrelevant information, handling missing values, and normalizing the data to ensure consistency.

Feature Extraction: Identifying the most relevant features or attributes from the data that can contribute to threat detection. For example, this may involve extracting specific user behaviors, network patterns, or file characteristics that are indicative of potential attacks.

Model Training: Utilizing machine learning algorithms to build predictive models based on the preprocessed data. These models learn from historical data to recognize patterns associated with cyber threats.

Threat Detection: Applying the trained models to new data to identify potential threats in real-time. When the model detects suspicious patterns, alerts are generated for further investigation.

Machine Learning Techniques for Data Mining

Several machine learning techniques can be employed for data mining in cybersecurity, each offering unique advantages:

Supervised Learning

In supervised learning, algorithms are trained on labeled datasets, where each data point is associated with a known outcome (e.g., benign or malicious). Common supervised learning algorithms include:

Decision Trees: These models use a tree-like structure to make decisions based on feature values. They are interpretable and can provide insights into the factors contributing to threat detection.

Random Forests: An ensemble method that combines multiple decision trees to improve accuracy and reduce overfitting. It is effective for handling complex datasets with many features.

Support Vector Machines (SVM): SVM algorithms aim to find the hyperplane that best separates different classes in the data. They are particularly useful for high-dimensional datasets.

Neural Networks: These models mimic the human brain's neural structure and can capture complex patterns in data. Deep learning, a subset of neural networks, has gained popularity in cybersecurity for analyzing large and unstructured datasets.

Unsupervised Learning

Unsupervised learning algorithms analyze unlabeled data to identify patterns and group similar data points. This approach is particularly useful for detecting anomalies that may indicate security threats. Common unsupervised learning techniques include:

Clustering Algorithms (e.g., K-Means, DBSCAN): These algorithms group similar data points together based on their features, helping to identify unusual patterns or outliers that may signify an attack.

Anomaly Detection Techniques: Algorithms like Isolation Forest and One-Class SVM are designed to detect anomalies in the data. They learn the normal behavior of the system and flag deviations as potential threats.

Semi-Supervised Learning

Semi-supervised learning combines labeled and unlabeled data to improve model performance. This technique is particularly beneficial in cybersecurity, where acquiring labeled data (e.g., identifying malware) can be challenging due to the constantly changing threat landscape. By leveraging both types of data, organizations can enhance their threat detection capabilities.

Real-World Applications of Data Mining for Cyber Threats

Intrusion Detection Systems (IDS)

Data mining techniques are commonly employed in IDS to monitor network traffic and identify potential intrusions. For example, machine learning algorithms can analyze patterns in network packets and flag anomalies that deviate from normal behavior, alerting security teams to potential breaches.

Phishing Detection

Phishing attacks remain a prevalent threat, and data mining can help organizations detect phishing attempts by analyzing email content, sender behavior, and user interactions. By identifying patterns associated with phishing emails, organizations can filter out malicious messages before they reach users.

Malware Classification

Machine learning models can analyze the characteristics of files and programs to classify them as benign or malicious. By training models on large datasets of known malware samples, organizations can improve their ability to detect and block new malware strains.

User Behavior Analytics (UBA)

UBA solutions leverage data mining techniques to monitor user activities and identify deviations from normal behavior. By establishing baseline profiles for users, organizations can detect insider threats or compromised accounts based on unusual patterns of access or behavior.

Threat Intelligence

Data mining can enhance threat intelligence by aggregating and analyzing data from multiple sources, such as security blogs, threat feeds, and social media. Machine learning algorithms can extract valuable insights from this data, helping organizations stay informed about emerging threats and vulnerabilities.

Benefits of Data Mining for Cyber Threats

Proactive Threat Detection

Data mining enables organizations to shift from reactive to proactive threat detection. By identifying patterns and anomalies in real-time, organizations can mitigate threats before they escalate into full-blown incidents.

Enhanced Decision-Making

Machine learning models provide security teams with actionable insights, enabling them to make informed decisions during incident response. The ability to analyze vast amounts of data quickly helps teams prioritize threats and allocate resources effectively.

Reduced False Positives

Advanced data mining techniques can reduce the number of false positives generated by traditional security systems. By leveraging machine learning algorithms, organizations can refine their detection capabilities, minimizing unnecessary alerts and focusing on genuine threats.

Scalability

As organizations grow and the volume of data increases, data mining techniques can scale to handle large datasets efficiently. Machine learning algorithms can adapt to evolving data patterns, ensuring ongoing effectiveness in threat detection.

Challenges of Data Mining for Cyber Threats

Data Quality and Diversity

The success of data mining relies heavily on the quality and diversity of the data being analyzed. Incomplete or biased datasets can lead to inaccurate predictions and threat assessments. Organizations must ensure that their data sources are comprehensive and representative of the threat landscape.

Complexity of Algorithms

While machine learning algorithms offer powerful capabilities, they can also be complex and require specialized knowledge to implement and maintain. Organizations may face challenges in recruiting skilled data scientists and cybersecurity professionals capable of managing these technologies.

Evolving Threat Landscape

Cyber threats are constantly evolving, and machine learning models trained on historical data may struggle to detect new attack vectors. Continuous training and updating of models are necessary to ensure their effectiveness against emerging threats.

Privacy Concerns

Data mining often involves analyzing sensitive information, raising privacy and compliance concerns. Organizations must ensure that their data mining practices adhere to relevant regulations and ethical standards to protect user privacy.

Data mining through machine learning presents a powerful approach to extracting insights from the vast amounts of data generated in cybersecurity. By leveraging advanced algorithms and techniques, organizations can proactively identify cyber threats, enhance decision-making, and strengthen their overall security posture. While challenges such as data quality, algorithm complexity, and evolving threats exist, the benefits of data mining for cyber threats far outweigh the drawbacks. As cybercriminals continue to innovate, organizations that embrace data mining techniques will be better equipped to defend against increasingly sophisticated attacks. By integrating machine learning into their cybersecurity strategies, organizations can unlock the full potential of their data and enhance their resilience against cyber threats.

5.2 Predictive Models: How Machine Learning Anticipates Future Attacks

In the dynamic world of cybersecurity, anticipating future attacks is essential for protecting organizations against evolving threats. As cybercriminals become increasingly sophisticated, traditional reactive approaches to security are often inadequate. This is where predictive models powered by machine learning (ML) come into play. By leveraging historical data and advanced algorithms, predictive models can identify patterns and trends, enabling organizations to foresee potential security breaches before they occur. This section delves into the mechanisms behind predictive models in cybersecurity, their applications, and the benefits they offer in the fight against cyber threats.

Understanding Predictive Models in Cybersecurity

Predictive modeling is a statistical technique that uses historical data to forecast future outcomes. In cybersecurity, predictive models analyze data from past incidents, user behaviors, and system vulnerabilities to make informed predictions about potential future attacks. These models can identify risk factors, detect anomalies, and prioritize threats, allowing organizations to allocate resources effectively and implement proactive defense measures.

The predictive modeling process generally involves the following steps:

Data Collection: Gathering relevant data from various sources, such as network logs, incident reports, threat intelligence feeds, and user behavior analytics. This data serves as the foundation for building predictive models.

Data Preprocessing: Cleaning and preparing the data for analysis. This includes removing irrelevant information, handling missing values, and normalizing the data to ensure consistency.

Feature Selection: Identifying the most relevant features or attributes from the dataset that contribute to predicting future attacks. Features may include specific behaviors, system configurations, or known vulnerabilities.

Model Selection and Training: Choosing appropriate machine learning algorithms (e.g., decision trees, random forests, or neural networks) and training the model on historical data. During this phase, the model learns to recognize patterns associated with previous attacks.

Model Evaluation: Assessing the accuracy and effectiveness of the predictive model using metrics such as precision, recall, and F1 score. This step ensures that the model can generalize well to new data.

Deployment and Monitoring: Implementing the predictive model in real-time environments, where it continuously analyzes incoming data to identify potential threats. Ongoing monitoring and updating of the model are crucial for maintaining its effectiveness.

Types of Predictive Models Used in Cybersecurity

Regression Models

Regression models predict continuous outcomes based on historical data. In cybersecurity, regression analysis can be used to estimate the likelihood of an attack occurring within a specific timeframe based on various risk factors. For example, logistic regression can help assess the probability of a user falling victim to phishing based on their behavior and characteristics.

Classification Models

Classification models categorize data points into predefined classes. In cybersecurity, these models can be employed to classify network traffic as benign or malicious based on historical patterns. Common classification algorithms include:

Decision Trees: These models use a tree-like structure to make decisions based on feature values. They are interpretable and can highlight the factors leading to a specific classification.

Random Forests: An ensemble method that combines multiple decision trees, random forests improve accuracy and reduce overfitting by aggregating predictions from several models.

Support Vector Machines (SVM): SVMs aim to find the optimal hyperplane that separates different classes in the data. They are effective in high-dimensional spaces, making them suitable for complex cybersecurity datasets.

Neural Networks: Deep learning models can capture intricate patterns in large datasets, making them ideal for identifying complex threats and predicting future attacks.

Anomaly Detection Models

Anomaly detection models identify data points that deviate from established norms. In cybersecurity, these models can help detect unusual behavior indicative of potential threats. For instance, unsupervised learning techniques such as clustering can uncover abnormal patterns in user activity, alerting security teams to possible breaches.

Applications of Predictive Models in Cybersecurity

Threat Intelligence and Risk Assessment

Predictive models can enhance threat intelligence by analyzing historical attack data to identify trends and emerging threats. By recognizing patterns in past attacks, organizations can assess their risk levels and prioritize defense strategies accordingly.

User Behavior Analytics (UBA)

Predictive modeling is widely used in UBA to establish baseline user behaviors and detect deviations that may indicate compromised accounts or insider threats. By analyzing user activity over time, organizations can proactively identify and respond to potential threats.

Vulnerability Management

Organizations can use predictive models to assess vulnerabilities within their systems and predict which vulnerabilities are most likely to be exploited. This proactive approach enables security teams to prioritize patching efforts and implement targeted security measures.

Phishing Detection

Predictive models can analyze email characteristics, sender behavior, and user interactions to predict the likelihood of phishing attempts. By identifying emails with a high probability of being phishing attempts, organizations can filter out harmful messages before they reach users.

Intrusion Detection Systems (IDS)

Predictive models can enhance IDS by analyzing network traffic patterns and identifying potential intrusions in real time. By continuously monitoring network activity, these models can predict and flag unusual behaviors that may indicate an ongoing attack.

Benefits of Predictive Models in Cybersecurity

Proactive Threat Detection

Predictive models empower organizations to shift from a reactive stance to a proactive approach in threat detection. By anticipating potential attacks, organizations can implement preventative measures before incidents occur.

Improved Resource Allocation

By identifying high-risk areas and predicting potential attacks, organizations can allocate resources more effectively. This targeted approach helps ensure that security teams focus on the most critical threats, optimizing their response efforts.

Enhanced Incident Response

Predictive models provide valuable insights that can inform incident response strategies. By understanding the likely tactics, techniques, and procedures (TTPs) employed by attackers, organizations can develop tailored response plans that address specific threats.

Reduced Attack Surface

By predicting potential attack vectors and prioritizing remediation efforts, organizations can reduce their overall attack surface. Proactive measures such as patching vulnerabilities and implementing security controls help mitigate risks before they can be exploited.

Continuous Improvement

Predictive models evolve over time as they learn from new data and threats. This continuous improvement ensures that organizations remain resilient in the face of an ever-changing threat landscape.

Challenges of Implementing Predictive Models in Cybersecurity

Data Quality and Availability

The accuracy of predictive models relies heavily on the quality and availability of historical data. Incomplete or biased datasets can lead to inaccurate predictions and misinterpretations of threat levels.

Model Complexity

Building and maintaining predictive models can be complex and require specialized knowledge in data science and machine learning. Organizations may face challenges in recruiting skilled professionals to develop and manage these models effectively.

Evolving Threat Landscape

The rapid evolution of cyber threats poses a challenge for predictive models. Attackers continuously adapt their tactics, requiring organizations to regularly update and retrain their models to maintain effectiveness.

False Positives and Negatives

Predictive models may generate false positives (incorrectly flagging benign activity as a threat) or false negatives (failing to detect actual threats). Balancing sensitivity and specificity is crucial for effective threat detection.

Privacy Concerns

The use of predictive models may raise privacy concerns, particularly when analyzing user data. Organizations must ensure compliance with data protection regulations and prioritize user privacy while leveraging predictive analytics.

Predictive models powered by machine learning have revolutionized the field of cybersecurity, enabling organizations to anticipate future attacks and proactively strengthen their defenses. By analyzing historical data, identifying patterns, and predicting potential threats, these models empower security teams to allocate resources effectively, enhance incident response, and ultimately reduce the risk of cyber incidents.

While challenges such as data quality, model complexity, and evolving threats exist, the benefits of implementing predictive models far outweigh the drawbacks. As cybercriminals continue to innovate and adapt their tactics, organizations that leverage predictive analytics will be better positioned to defend against sophisticated attacks and ensure the security of their digital assets. By embracing predictive modeling, organizations can enhance their cybersecurity strategies and create a resilient defense against the ever-changing landscape of cyber threats.

5.3 Big Data in Cybersecurity: The Role of AI in Managing Massive Datasets

In the contemporary landscape of cybersecurity, the sheer volume and complexity of data generated daily present both challenges and opportunities. Organizations across various sectors accumulate vast amounts of data from diverse sources, including network logs, user activity, threat intelligence feeds, and application transactions. This explosion of data—often referred to as "big data"—is both a boon for cybersecurity professionals and a significant hurdle in identifying and mitigating threats. Artificial Intelligence (AI) plays a crucial role in effectively managing these massive datasets, enabling organizations to extract actionable insights, enhance threat detection capabilities, and respond swiftly to potential attacks. This section explores the intersection of big data and AI in cybersecurity, focusing on the methodologies, benefits, and challenges associated with leveraging AI to manage and analyze large datasets.

Understanding Big Data in Cybersecurity

Big data refers to datasets that are characterized by their volume, variety, velocity, and veracity—commonly known as the "Four Vs." In cybersecurity, these dimensions manifest in the following ways:

Volume: The sheer amount of data generated by organizations is staggering. For example, security logs from firewalls, intrusion detection systems, and endpoint devices can accumulate terabytes of information daily. This data must be processed and analyzed to identify potential threats.

Variety: Cybersecurity data comes in various forms, including structured data (e.g., log files, databases) and unstructured data (e.g., emails, social media posts). Different types of data require diverse analytical techniques, making it challenging to gain a comprehensive view of the security landscape.

Velocity: The speed at which data is generated and needs to be processed is critical. Cyberattacks can occur within seconds, necessitating real-time analysis to identify and mitigate threats effectively.

Veracity: The reliability and accuracy of the data are paramount. Organizations must ensure that the data they analyze is trustworthy to avoid false positives and negatives in threat detection.

Given these challenges, organizations must adopt robust strategies to manage big data effectively. AI technologies, particularly machine learning and data analytics, have emerged as powerful tools to process and analyze vast datasets in cybersecurity.

The Role of AI in Managing Big Data

Data Collection and Integration

AI facilitates the automated collection and integration of data from multiple sources, enabling organizations to compile a comprehensive dataset for analysis. This process may involve aggregating logs from various systems, correlating threat intelligence feeds, and unifying data from cloud environments, on-premises networks, and endpoint devices. By leveraging AI-driven data collection tools, organizations can streamline their data aggregation processes, ensuring they have access to the most relevant information for threat detection.

Data Preprocessing and Cleaning

Before analyzing data, organizations must preprocess and clean it to ensure accuracy and consistency. AI algorithms can automate data cleaning tasks, such as identifying and removing duplicates, handling missing values, and normalizing formats. By employing natural language processing (NLP) techniques, AI can also analyze unstructured data (e.g., text logs) to extract relevant information and insights.

Real-Time Analysis and Threat Detection

One of the most significant advantages of AI in cybersecurity is its ability to analyze data in real-time. Machine learning algorithms can continuously monitor network traffic, user behavior, and system logs to detect anomalies indicative of potential attacks. By establishing baselines for normal behavior, these algorithms can flag deviations that warrant investigation, allowing security teams to respond swiftly to emerging threats.

Predictive Analytics

Predictive analytics, powered by AI, enables organizations to forecast potential threats based on historical data patterns. By analyzing trends and behaviors associated with past attacks, predictive models can anticipate future threats and prioritize vulnerabilities that require immediate attention. This proactive approach allows organizations to implement preventive measures and reduce their attack surface.

Automated Incident Response

AI can enhance incident response by automating various tasks involved in threat mitigation. For instance, AI-driven security orchestration, automation, and response (SOAR) platforms can analyze alerts, correlate incidents, and initiate automated responses, such as blocking malicious IP addresses or isolating compromised endpoints. This automation reduces response times and minimizes the impact of attacks.

Threat Intelligence and Behavioral Analytics

AI plays a vital role in analyzing threat intelligence feeds and behavioral data to identify patterns associated with cyber threats. By correlating data from various sources, AI can provide organizations with actionable insights that inform their security strategies. Behavioral analytics, powered by machine learning, allows organizations to understand user and entity behavior, helping them identify suspicious activities that may indicate compromised accounts or insider threats.

Benefits of AI in Big Data Management for Cybersecurity

Enhanced Threat Detection

AI algorithms can sift through vast amounts of data quickly and accurately, significantly improving the ability to detect potential threats. By analyzing data patterns and anomalies, organizations can identify and respond to security incidents in real time, reducing the likelihood of data breaches.

Increased Efficiency and Speed

Automating data collection, preprocessing, and analysis with AI enables security teams to focus their efforts on strategic decision-making rather than manual data handling. This increased efficiency leads to faster identification of threats and a more agile security posture.

Improved Decision-Making

AI-driven analytics provide security teams with actionable insights and recommendations based on data-driven evidence. By leveraging these insights, organizations can make informed decisions regarding their cybersecurity strategies and resource allocation.

Scalability

As organizations grow and their data volumes increase, AI can scale to accommodate larger datasets without sacrificing performance. This scalability ensures that organizations can maintain effective security measures even in the face of increasing data complexity.

Cost-Effectiveness

By automating data management and threat detection processes, AI can help organizations reduce operational costs associated with manual monitoring and analysis. This cost-effectiveness allows organizations to allocate resources more effectively across their cybersecurity programs.

Challenges of Using AI for Big Data Management in Cybersecurity

Data Privacy and Compliance

The use of AI to analyze large datasets raises concerns regarding data privacy and compliance with regulations such as GDPR or CCPA. Organizations must ensure that their AI-driven processes respect user privacy and adhere to legal requirements when handling sensitive data.

False Positives and Negatives

While AI improves threat detection capabilities, there is still the risk of false positives (innocuous activities flagged as threats) and false negatives (real threats going undetected). Striking the right balance in model sensitivity is critical to maintaining effective security without overwhelming security teams with unnecessary alerts.

Complexity of Implementation

Integrating AI solutions into existing cybersecurity frameworks can be complex and may require significant investments in infrastructure, training, and expertise. Organizations may face challenges in selecting the right AI tools and technologies that align with their specific security needs.

Skill Gap and Resource Requirements

The successful deployment of AI in cybersecurity requires skilled professionals who can manage AI technologies, interpret results, and make informed decisions based on data insights. Organizations may struggle to find and retain talent with the necessary expertise to leverage AI effectively.

Adversarial Attacks on AI Models

Cybercriminals are increasingly targeting AI systems with adversarial attacks designed to manipulate or deceive machine learning models. These attacks can undermine the effectiveness of AI-driven security solutions, making it crucial for organizations to implement robust defenses against such threats.

The integration of big data and artificial intelligence has transformed the field of cybersecurity, enabling organizations to manage and analyze massive datasets more effectively. AI's capabilities in data collection, preprocessing, real-time analysis, predictive analytics, and automated incident response significantly enhance organizations' ability to detect and mitigate cyber threats.

While challenges such as data privacy, implementation complexity, and the skill gap exist, the benefits of leveraging AI to manage big data in cybersecurity far outweigh the drawbacks. As the threat landscape continues to evolve, organizations that embrace AI-driven solutions will be better equipped to navigate the complexities of big data and enhance their overall security posture. By harnessing the power of AI, organizations can turn their big data challenges into opportunities for improved threat detection, incident response, and resilience against cyber attacks.

Chapter 6: The Role of Natural Language Processing (NLP) in Cybersecurity

In this chapter, we delve into the pivotal role of Natural Language Processing (NLP) in enhancing cybersecurity measures. As cyber threats increasingly exploit human vulnerabilities, particularly through social engineering tactics like phishing, NLP emerges as a powerful tool to analyze and understand human language. We begin by exploring how NLP techniques can be utilized to detect malicious communications, such as phishing emails and deceptive messages, by examining linguistic patterns and contextual cues. Additionally, we discuss the application of NLP in monitoring dark web forums and social media platforms to gather intelligence on emerging threats and criminal activities. The chapter also addresses the challenges and limitations of NLP in cybersecurity, including the complexity of language and the potential for adversarial attacks against NLP models. By harnessing the capabilities of NLP, organizations can significantly enhance their threat detection capabilities and strengthen their defenses against increasingly sophisticated cyber threats, making it an invaluable component of modern cybersecurity strategies.

6.1 Phishing Detection: Using NLP to Identify Malicious Emails

Phishing attacks have become one of the most prevalent and damaging forms of cybercrime. Cybercriminals use phishing techniques to deceive individuals into divulging sensitive information, such as login credentials, financial details, or personal data, by masquerading as trustworthy entities. These attacks can take many forms, including emails, text messages, and websites that look legitimate but are designed to steal information. Given the sophistication of modern phishing tactics, traditional security measures often fall short. This is where Natural Language Processing (NLP), a branch of artificial intelligence, plays a crucial role in enhancing phishing detection capabilities. This section explores how NLP can be employed to identify and mitigate phishing attempts in email communications, thereby strengthening cybersecurity defenses.

Understanding Phishing Attacks

Phishing attacks typically involve fraudulent emails that aim to trick recipients into taking specific actions, such as clicking on a malicious link or downloading an infected attachment. These emails often exhibit certain characteristics, including:

Urgency: Phishing emails frequently create a sense of urgency, prompting the recipient to act quickly without considering the legitimacy of the message. Phrases like "Immediate action required" or "Your account will be suspended" are common.

Spoofed Sender Addresses: Attackers often use email addresses that resemble legitimate ones but contain slight variations, making them appear credible at first glance.

Generic Greetings: Phishing emails typically lack personalization, using generic greetings such as "Dear Customer" instead of the recipient's name.

Suspicious Links and Attachments: Malicious emails often contain hyperlinks that lead to fraudulent websites or attachments that, when opened, can install malware on the victim's device.

Given these tactics, there is a pressing need for advanced methods to detect phishing emails effectively. NLP, with its ability to analyze and understand human language, provides powerful tools to identify the subtle cues indicative of phishing attempts.

The Role of Natural Language Processing in Phishing Detection

NLP encompasses a range of techniques that allow computers to process, analyze, and understand human language. In the context of phishing detection, NLP can be employed in various ways to enhance the identification of malicious emails:

Text Classification

One of the primary applications of NLP in phishing detection is text classification, where algorithms are trained to categorize emails as either "phishing" or "legitimate." Machine learning models, such as support vector machines, decision trees, and neural networks, can be used for this purpose. The models analyze features derived from the email's content, including:

Word Frequency Analysis: NLP techniques can analyze the frequency of specific words or phrases commonly associated with phishing attacks, such as "urgent," "verify," or "account."

TF-IDF (Term Frequency-Inverse Document Frequency): This statistical measure evaluates the importance of a word in a document relative to a collection of documents.

Words that are frequently used in phishing emails but rarely in legitimate emails can be identified as potential indicators of malicious intent.

Sentiment Analysis

Phishing emails often employ emotional language to manipulate recipients into taking action. NLP can be used to perform sentiment analysis on email content, allowing algorithms to detect overly negative or urgent sentiments indicative of phishing. For instance, messages with alarming phrases or threats of account suspension may raise red flags.

Entity Recognition

Named Entity Recognition (NER) is an NLP technique that identifies and classifies entities in text, such as people, organizations, dates, and locations. By analyzing emails for the presence of unusual or irrelevant entities, NLP can help identify potentially fraudulent content. For example, an email claiming to be from a bank but referencing a generic financial service could be flagged for further investigation.

Contextual Understanding

Advanced NLP models, such as those based on transformers (e.g., BERT, GPT), are capable of understanding the context of words within sentences. This contextual understanding allows models to capture nuances in language that may indicate phishing attempts. For example, an email that uses formal language and proper grammar but contains suspicious requests can be flagged as potentially harmful.

Link and Attachment Analysis

In addition to analyzing the text content of emails, NLP can be used in conjunction with other techniques to examine embedded links and attachments. For instance, the URLs in emails can be checked against known malicious domains, and attachments can be scanned for malware. By combining text analysis with link and attachment scrutiny, organizations can enhance their phishing detection capabilities significantly.

Implementation of NLP-Based Phishing Detection Systems

To implement NLP-based phishing detection systems effectively, organizations should consider the following steps:

Data Collection and Labeling

The first step in building an NLP model for phishing detection is collecting a substantial dataset of both phishing and legitimate emails. This dataset should be labeled to indicate whether each email is malicious or benign, serving as the training data for machine learning algorithms.

Feature Engineering

Once the data is collected, feature engineering involves selecting and transforming relevant features from the raw text for analysis. This process may include tokenization (breaking text into words or phrases), removing stop words (common words that add little meaning), and applying techniques such as stemming or lemmatization (reducing words to their root forms).

Model Training

After preprocessing the data, organizations can train machine learning models using various algorithms, such as logistic regression, random forests, or deep learning approaches like recurrent neural networks (RNNs) or convolutional neural networks (CNNs). The models learn to recognize patterns associated with phishing emails based on the labeled training data.

Model Evaluation and Optimization

The trained model must be evaluated using a separate validation dataset to assess its performance. Key evaluation metrics include accuracy, precision, recall, and F1 score. Organizations can refine their models by tuning hyperparameters, adjusting feature selection, or experimenting with different algorithms to improve detection rates.

Deployment and Monitoring

Once the model achieves satisfactory performance, it can be deployed in a real-time environment, where it analyzes incoming emails for phishing indicators. Continuous monitoring is essential to ensure the model remains effective as phishing tactics evolve over time. Organizations should periodically retrain the model with new data to adapt to changing threat landscapes.

Benefits of Using NLP for Phishing Detection

Increased Detection Accuracy

By leveraging NLP techniques, organizations can significantly enhance the accuracy of their phishing detection systems. NLP's ability to analyze language patterns and sentiments allows for the identification of subtle cues that may indicate malicious intent.

Scalability

NLP algorithms can efficiently process large volumes of emails, making them suitable for organizations of all sizes. As email traffic grows, NLP-based systems can scale to handle increasing workloads without sacrificing performance.

Real-Time Analysis

NLP-based phishing detection systems can analyze emails in real time, enabling organizations to respond swiftly to potential threats. This proactive approach reduces the risk of users falling victim to phishing attacks.

Reduction in False Positives

By employing advanced NLP techniques, organizations can minimize the occurrence of false positives, where legitimate emails are incorrectly flagged as phishing attempts. This reduction leads to improved user trust and satisfaction.

Continuous Learning

NLP models can adapt and learn from new data over time, ensuring that phishing detection capabilities remain effective as attackers develop new tactics. Continuous training helps organizations stay ahead of emerging threats.

Challenges of NLP in Phishing Detection

Complexity of Language

Human language is inherently complex and can be challenging for algorithms to understand fully. Sarcasm, idioms, and context-dependent meanings can lead to misinterpretations, resulting in missed detections or false positives.

Evolving Phishing Techniques

Cybercriminals constantly evolve their tactics to bypass detection systems. As phishing techniques become more sophisticated, NLP models must continuously adapt to maintain their effectiveness.

Data Quality and Availability

The success of NLP models relies on the quality and diversity of training data. Organizations may face challenges in obtaining sufficient labeled data to train their models accurately.

Resource Requirements

Implementing NLP-based phishing detection systems may require substantial computational resources and expertise in machine learning and natural language processing. Organizations may need to invest in specialized tools and personnel.

Privacy Concerns

Analyzing email content raises privacy concerns, particularly when dealing with sensitive information. Organizations must ensure compliance with data protection regulations and prioritize user privacy in their phishing detection efforts.

Phishing attacks remain a significant threat in the digital age, necessitating advanced detection mechanisms to protect individuals and organizations from malicious actors. Natural Language Processing (NLP) offers powerful tools to enhance phishing detection capabilities by analyzing the language patterns, sentiments, and contextual cues present in emails. By leveraging NLP techniques, organizations can build effective phishing detection systems that significantly reduce the risk of falling victim to these pervasive attacks.

While challenges exist, such as the complexity of language and the evolving tactics of cybercriminals, the benefits of implementing NLP-based solutions far outweigh the drawbacks. As organizations continue to adopt AI-driven approaches to cybersecurity, NLP will play a pivotal role in enhancing email security, safeguarding sensitive information, and fostering a more resilient digital environment. By investing in NLP technologies, organizations can proactively defend against phishing attacks and protect their users from potential harm.

6.2 Analyzing Dark Web Communications with AI-Driven NLP

The dark web, a hidden part of the internet that is not indexed by traditional search engines, is notorious for its anonymity and illegal activities, including drug trafficking, weapons sales, and the distribution of stolen data. While the dark web poses significant threats to cybersecurity, it also provides valuable insights into emerging cyber threats, trends, and criminal networks. Analyzing communications on the dark web can help law enforcement, security agencies, and organizations anticipate attacks, understand threat actor motivations, and bolster their defense strategies. AI-driven Natural Language Processing (NLP) plays a crucial role in enabling effective analysis of dark web communications, allowing for the extraction of meaningful information from unstructured data. This section explores how AI-powered NLP techniques can be applied to analyze dark web communications and enhance cybersecurity efforts.

Understanding Dark Web Communications

Dark web communications often take place in forums, marketplaces, and chat rooms where anonymity is prioritized. Participants frequently use pseudonyms and encrypted messaging to protect their identities, making it challenging to track criminal activity. The nature of the communications can vary widely, including:

- **Market Listings**: Vendors advertising illegal goods or services, often using coded language to avoid detection.
- **Forum Discussions**: Users sharing information, techniques, or strategies related to hacking, malware development, or other illicit activities.
- **Threat Exchanges**: Criminals discussing potential targets, sharing exploit techniques, or offering services for hire.

Analyzing this communications landscape requires sophisticated techniques to navigate the unique challenges posed by the dark web, including the volume of data, anonymity of participants, and the unstructured nature of the text.

The Role of AI-Driven NLP in Analyzing Dark Web Communications

AI-driven NLP can facilitate the analysis of dark web communications in several key ways, enabling organizations to uncover insights and enhance their cybersecurity posture:

Data Collection and Scraping

The first step in analyzing dark web communications involves collecting data from various sources, including forums, marketplaces, and chat rooms. NLP tools can automate the scraping process, extracting relevant text data while maintaining anonymity. This process may involve:

- **Web Crawling**: Automated scripts can navigate dark web sites to gather content, extracting text, links, and metadata.
- **Natural Language Processing Techniques**: NLP can help identify relevant topics and categorize the data collected, enabling more focused analysis.

Text Preprocessing

The unstructured nature of dark web communications presents challenges for analysis. NLP techniques can preprocess this text to make it suitable for analysis, including:

- **Tokenization**: Breaking down text into individual words or phrases for further analysis.
- **Removing Stop Words**: Filtering out common words (e.g., "and," "the") that do not contribute meaningful information.
- **Stemming and Lemmatization**: Reducing words to their base or root forms, allowing for more accurate analysis across variations of words.

Sentiment Analysis

Sentiment analysis, an NLP technique, can be employed to assess the emotions and opinions expressed in dark web communications. By analyzing the tone of discussions, organizations can gain insights into the motivations of threat actors and the overall mood within criminal communities. For example:

- **Positive Sentiments**: Indicate satisfaction with successful operations or the performance of a particular tool or service.
- **Negative Sentiments**: Reveal frustration or dissatisfaction with failed attacks or law enforcement activities.

Topic Modeling

Topic modeling is an NLP technique that identifies themes or topics within large collections of text. By applying algorithms such as Latent Dirichlet Allocation (LDA), organizations can uncover prevalent subjects discussed on the dark web. This information can help identify emerging threats and areas of interest within criminal networks, such as:

- **Commonly Discussed Exploits**: Identifying popular vulnerabilities being targeted by threat actors.
- **Emerging Trends**: Recognizing shifts in criminal behavior or new types of illicit goods being offered.

Named Entity Recognition (NER)

Named Entity Recognition is an NLP technique that identifies and classifies entities within text, such as people, organizations, locations, and dates. In the context of dark web communications, NER can help:

- **Identify Key Players**: Recognize individuals or groups involved in criminal activities, enabling better understanding of networks.
- **Track Goods and Services**: Monitor mentions of specific illegal goods or services, assisting law enforcement in targeting operations.

Anomaly Detection

Anomaly detection techniques can be applied to identify unusual patterns or behaviors in dark web communications. For instance, organizations can analyze communication volumes, frequency of posts, or the emergence of new topics to detect potential threats or shifts in criminal activity. By establishing baselines for normal behavior, organizations can flag deviations that warrant further investigation.

Translation and Language Processing

The dark web encompasses a diverse range of languages and dialects, making communication analysis more complex. AI-driven NLP models can automatically translate and process multilingual text, allowing organizations to analyze communications regardless of language barriers. This capability enables a more comprehensive understanding of global criminal networks and their activities.

Implementation of AI-Driven NLP in Dark Web Analysis

To implement AI-driven NLP for analyzing dark web communications effectively, organizations should follow a structured approach:

Define Objectives

Organizations must clearly define their objectives for analyzing dark web communications. These objectives may include monitoring for specific threats, understanding criminal trends, or identifying potential targets for law enforcement operations.

Data Collection Framework

Establishing a robust data collection framework is crucial for effective analysis. Organizations can utilize web scraping tools and automated scripts to gather data from dark web sources while maintaining compliance with legal and ethical standards.

NLP Model Development

Organizations should develop NLP models tailored to their specific analysis needs. This may involve training machine learning models on relevant datasets to enhance accuracy and effectiveness. Common approaches include supervised learning for classification tasks and unsupervised learning for topic modeling.

Continuous Learning and Adaptation

Dark web communications are constantly evolving, and threat actors frequently change their tactics. Organizations must implement continuous learning strategies to ensure their NLP models remain effective. This may involve regularly updating datasets, retraining models, and adapting to new language patterns or slang.

Collaboration with Law Enforcement

Collaboration with law enforcement and intelligence agencies can enhance the effectiveness of dark web analysis. Sharing insights and findings can lead to coordinated efforts to dismantle criminal networks and disrupt illicit activities.

Ethical Considerations

Analyzing dark web communications raises ethical considerations, particularly concerning user privacy and data protection. Organizations must adhere to legal regulations and ethical guidelines when collecting and analyzing data from the dark web, ensuring that their efforts do not infringe on individual rights.

Benefits of AI-Driven NLP in Dark Web Analysis

Proactive Threat Detection

By leveraging AI-driven NLP, organizations can proactively identify emerging threats on the dark web. This proactive stance enables security teams to stay ahead of potential attacks and mitigate risks before they materialize.

Enhanced Situational Awareness

Analyzing dark web communications provides organizations with a deeper understanding of the threat landscape. This situational awareness informs security strategies and allows for more effective resource allocation.

Data-Driven Decision Making

AI-driven insights from dark web analysis empower organizations to make data-driven decisions regarding their cybersecurity posture. By understanding the tactics and motivations of threat actors, organizations can tailor their defenses accordingly.

Collaboration Opportunities

Insights gleaned from dark web communications can foster collaboration between organizations and law enforcement agencies. Sharing information about threats and criminal activities can lead to more effective investigations and interventions.

Resource Optimization

Automating the analysis of dark web communications with AI-driven NLP allows organizations to allocate human resources more effectively. Security teams can focus their efforts on higher-priority tasks, such as responding to identified threats or improving overall security posture.

Challenges of Using AI-Driven NLP for Dark Web Analysis

Anonymity and Obfuscation

The dark web's emphasis on anonymity presents challenges in tracing individuals and understanding networks. While NLP can analyze communications, determining the actual identities of threat actors remains complex.

Volume and Complexity of Data

The sheer volume of data generated on the dark web can be overwhelming. Organizations must develop scalable solutions to process and analyze this data efficiently.

Dynamic Nature of Threats

Threats on the dark web are dynamic and constantly evolving. NLP models must adapt to these changes to remain effective, requiring continuous updates and retraining.

Legal and Ethical Concerns

Engaging with the dark web raises legal and ethical questions regarding data privacy and compliance. Organizations must navigate these challenges carefully to avoid potential legal ramifications.

Skill Gap and Resource Requirements

Implementing AI-driven NLP solutions requires specialized skills and expertise in machine learning, data science, and cybersecurity. Organizations may need to invest in training or hire skilled personnel to manage these technologies effectively.

AI-driven Natural Language Processing (NLP) represents a powerful tool for analyzing dark web communications, enabling organizations to uncover valuable insights and enhance their cybersecurity defenses. By leveraging NLP techniques such as data collection, sentiment analysis, topic modeling, and named entity recognition, organizations can proactively identify emerging threats, understand criminal motivations, and stay ahead of potential attacks.

While challenges such as anonymity, data volume, and legal considerations exist, the benefits of utilizing AI-driven NLP for dark web analysis far outweigh the drawbacks. As the threat landscape continues to evolve, organizations that invest in these technologies will be better equipped to navigate the complexities of the dark web, protect sensitive information, and contribute to a safer digital environment. By harnessing the power of AI and NLP, organizations can enhance their ability to analyze dark web communications and ultimately strengthen their overall cybersecurity posture.

6.3 NLP for Social Engineering Defense: Understanding Deceptive Language Patterns

Social engineering remains one of the most insidious forms of cyber threats, as it exploits human psychology rather than relying solely on technical vulnerabilities. Attackers manipulate individuals into divulging sensitive information or performing actions that compromise security, often using deceptive language and psychological tactics. The subtlety of these attacks makes them challenging to detect and prevent. However, advancements in Natural Language Processing (NLP) offer new avenues for defending against social engineering attempts by analyzing and understanding the linguistic patterns commonly associated with deception. This section explores how NLP can be leveraged to identify and mitigate social engineering threats by examining deceptive language patterns.

Understanding Social Engineering Attacks

Social engineering attacks can take many forms, including phishing emails, phone scams, pretexting, and baiting. The attackers craft messages that create a sense of urgency, fear, or trust, manipulating victims into acting against their best interests. Key characteristics of social engineering language include:

Urgent Calls to Action: Attackers often create a sense of urgency to prompt immediate responses, using phrases like "Act now!" or "Your account will be suspended!"

Authority Appeals: Many social engineering attempts involve impersonating authority figures, such as IT personnel or bank representatives, to gain the victim's trust.

Ambiguity and Vagueness: Attackers may use ambiguous language to confuse victims, leaving them unsure about the legitimacy of the request.

Personalization: Many social engineering messages are tailored to the individual, using personal information to establish credibility and rapport.

Understanding these patterns is crucial for developing effective defenses against social engineering attacks. NLP techniques can be employed to analyze and identify these deceptive language characteristics, helping organizations to implement proactive measures to protect against such threats.

The Role of NLP in Analyzing Deceptive Language Patterns

NLP encompasses various techniques that allow for the analysis of language patterns, sentiment, and context. When applied to the detection of deceptive language in social engineering, NLP can provide valuable insights and tools for defense mechanisms. Here are several key applications of NLP in this context:

Text Classification

Text classification algorithms can be employed to categorize messages as either legitimate or potentially deceptive. Machine learning models can be trained on labeled datasets containing examples of both types of messages, enabling the algorithms to learn distinguishing features. Features analyzed may include:

Word Choice and Frequency: Certain words or phrases may be more prevalent in deceptive messages. NLP can analyze the frequency of these indicators to assess the likelihood of deception.

Length of Messages: Deceptive messages may exhibit certain length patterns, such as unusually brief or excessively verbose content.

Sentiment Analysis

Sentiment analysis can be used to assess the emotional tone of messages. Many social engineering attacks rely on evoking strong emotions to manipulate the victim. By analyzing sentiment, organizations can flag messages that exhibit:

- **Negative Emotions**: Fear, anxiety, or urgency often indicate potential deception.
- **Overly Positive Language**: Messages that appear too good to be true, using exaggerated positive language, may also be suspect.

Discourse Analysis

Discourse analysis focuses on the structure and organization of language in communication. By analyzing the discourse patterns in messages, NLP can identify manipulative tactics, such as:

- **Logical Fallacies**: Attackers may employ logical fallacies to confuse or mislead victims. NLP can help identify these inconsistencies in reasoning.

- **Cohesion and Coherence**: Analyzing the flow of messages can reveal inconsistencies that may indicate deception, such as abrupt topic changes or contradictions.

Named Entity Recognition (NER)

NER techniques can identify entities mentioned in text, such as people, organizations, or dates. In social engineering contexts, analyzing the use of specific names or organizations can help identify:

- **Impersonation Attempts**: Messages that incorrectly reference well-known organizations or individuals may indicate a social engineering attack.
- **Unusual Contexts**: The presence of entities in unusual or irrelevant contexts can raise suspicion.

Language Modeling and Anomaly Detection

Language modeling techniques can be utilized to create profiles of typical communication patterns within an organization. By comparing incoming messages to these profiles, NLP can help detect anomalies that may suggest deceptive language, including:

- **Unusual Word Combinations**: Messages that utilize uncommon or unexpected word pairings may indicate deception.
- **Abnormal Syntax**: Deviations from typical sentence structures or grammar can also be indicators of suspicious communication.

Implementation of NLP for Social Engineering Defense

To effectively utilize NLP in defending against social engineering attacks, organizations should consider the following steps:

Data Collection and Labeling

The first step in developing NLP models is collecting a dataset of both deceptive and legitimate messages. This dataset should be labeled to indicate the nature of each message, providing the foundation for supervised machine learning approaches.

Feature Engineering

After collecting the data, organizations should perform feature engineering to extract relevant linguistic features. This process may involve identifying keywords, sentiment scores, and discourse patterns.

Model Development and Training

Organizations can develop machine learning models that leverage the extracted features for classification purposes. Common algorithms for this task include logistic regression, support vector machines, and neural networks. Training the models on the labeled dataset enables them to learn to identify deceptive patterns.

Evaluation and Optimization

Once the models are trained, they must be evaluated using a separate validation dataset to assess their accuracy and effectiveness. Key metrics for evaluation include precision, recall, and F1 score. Organizations should optimize the models by refining feature selection, tuning hyperparameters, or experimenting with different algorithms.

Deployment and Monitoring

After achieving satisfactory performance, the NLP model can be deployed to analyze incoming messages in real time. Continuous monitoring is essential to ensure the model remains effective as deceptive tactics evolve. Organizations should periodically retrain the model with new data to maintain accuracy.

Benefits of Using NLP for Social Engineering Defense

Enhanced Detection Capabilities

By leveraging NLP, organizations can significantly enhance their ability to detect social engineering attempts. NLP techniques can identify subtle linguistic cues that may be missed by traditional security measures.

Proactive Threat Mitigation

NLP-driven solutions enable organizations to proactively identify potential social engineering attacks before they can inflict damage. This proactive approach allows for timely intervention and mitigation of risks.

Improved User Awareness and Training

Insights gained from NLP analysis can be used to inform user training and awareness programs. By understanding the tactics used in social engineering attacks, organizations can educate employees on recognizing deceptive language patterns.

Resource Optimization

Automating the detection of social engineering attempts with NLP allows security teams to allocate their resources more effectively. By focusing on high-risk messages, organizations can optimize their response efforts.

Continuous Learning and Adaptation

NLP models can continuously learn from new data, adapting to evolving social engineering tactics. This adaptability is crucial in maintaining an effective defense against emerging threats.

Challenges of Using NLP for Social Engineering Defense

Complexity of Human Language

Human language is nuanced and context-dependent, making it challenging for algorithms to fully comprehend. Sarcasm, irony, and cultural references can complicate the detection of deception.

Evolving Tactics of Attackers

Cybercriminals constantly evolve their strategies to bypass detection systems. NLP models must be regularly updated to adapt to these changes and remain effective.

Data Quality and Availability

The effectiveness of NLP models relies on the quality and diversity of the training data. Organizations may face challenges in obtaining sufficient labeled data to train their models accurately.

Resource Requirements

Implementing NLP-driven solutions requires specialized skills and resources in machine learning, data analysis, and cybersecurity. Organizations may need to invest in training or hire skilled personnel to manage these technologies effectively.

Privacy and Ethical Considerations

Analyzing communication raises ethical concerns, particularly regarding user privacy. Organizations must ensure compliance with data protection regulations and prioritize ethical considerations in their social engineering defense efforts.

NLP offers a powerful approach to defending against social engineering attacks by analyzing deceptive language patterns and enhancing detection capabilities. By leveraging text classification, sentiment analysis, discourse analysis, and other NLP techniques, organizations can gain valuable insights into the tactics employed by attackers.

While challenges exist, such as the complexity of human language and the evolving nature of social engineering tactics, the benefits of utilizing NLP in social engineering defense far outweigh the drawbacks. Organizations that invest in NLP technologies will be better equipped to recognize and mitigate social engineering threats, ultimately enhancing their cybersecurity posture and safeguarding sensitive information. As social engineering attacks continue to evolve, the application of NLP will play a critical role in empowering organizations to stay one step ahead of cybercriminals and protect against the manipulative tactics that exploit human psychology.

Chapter 7: AI-Powered Security Operations Centers (SOCs)

In this chapter, we examine the evolution of Security Operations Centers (SOCs) through the integration of artificial intelligence, which is reshaping how organizations detect, analyze, and respond to cybersecurity incidents. As cyber threats become more sophisticated and frequent, traditional SOCs face challenges in managing the overwhelming volume of alerts and data. We explore how AI enhances SOC operations by automating routine tasks such as alert triage, incident prioritization, and data analysis, allowing security analysts to focus on more complex investigations. Furthermore, we discuss AI-assisted threat hunting, where machine learning algorithms proactively search for hidden threats within networks. This chapter also highlights real-world case studies demonstrating the effectiveness of AI in improving SOC efficiency and reducing response times. By embracing AI technologies, SOCs can evolve into smarter, more agile units capable of addressing the dynamic nature of cyber threats, ultimately strengthening an organization's overall security posture.

7.1 Automating Alert Triage and Response in SOCs

In today's digital landscape, Security Operations Centers (SOCs) serve as critical hubs for detecting, analyzing, and responding to cybersecurity incidents. However, the volume of alerts generated by various security tools can overwhelm SOC analysts, leading to alert fatigue and potential oversights. To address this challenge, organizations are increasingly turning to automation for alert triage and response. By leveraging automation technologies, SOCs can enhance their efficiency, reduce response times, and focus their human resources on more complex threats. This section explores how automating alert triage and response can transform SOC operations and improve overall cybersecurity posture.

Understanding Alert Triage in SOCs

Alert triage is the process of evaluating and prioritizing security alerts based on their severity, relevance, and potential impact on the organization. This process involves:

Categorization: Identifying the nature of the alert, whether it pertains to malware, unauthorized access, data exfiltration, or other threats.

Prioritization: Assessing the severity of the alert based on factors such as the sensitivity of the affected assets, the potential business impact, and the likelihood of a true positive.

Investigation: Conducting a preliminary investigation to determine whether the alert is a false positive or a legitimate threat requiring further action.

Response: Initiating appropriate response actions, which may include containment, remediation, or escalation to other teams.

In a traditional SOC environment, this triage process is often manual and time-consuming, resulting in delays and potential burnout among analysts. Automating these processes can significantly enhance SOC efficiency and effectiveness.

The Role of Automation in Alert Triage

Automation plays a crucial role in streamlining the alert triage process, providing several key benefits:

Reduction of Alert Overload

Automation tools can help manage the overwhelming volume of alerts generated by security systems. By applying predefined rules and machine learning algorithms, automated systems can filter out low-risk alerts and focus on those that require human attention. This reduction in alert noise allows analysts to concentrate on more critical incidents.

Enhanced Prioritization

Automated triage solutions can prioritize alerts based on risk factors and contextual data. For example, alerts related to sensitive data access may be prioritized over routine system updates. By integrating threat intelligence feeds and behavioral analytics, automation tools can assess the potential impact of each alert, ensuring that analysts focus on high-priority threats.

Consistency and Standardization

Human analysts may interpret alerts differently based on their experience and biases. Automation introduces consistency into the triage process, applying the same rules and criteria across all alerts. This standardization reduces the risk of human error and ensures a uniform approach to threat assessment.

Faster Response Times

Automated alert triage enables organizations to respond to threats more quickly. With real-time analysis and prioritization, SOC teams can initiate containment measures immediately, reducing the potential impact of an attack. Rapid response capabilities are critical in today's fast-paced threat landscape, where attackers can exploit vulnerabilities in minutes.

Data Enrichment

Automation tools can enrich alerts with contextual information, providing analysts with a comprehensive view of the threat landscape. For instance, integrating external threat intelligence can help identify known indicators of compromise (IOCs) associated with the alert, allowing for faster identification of threats and more informed decision-making.

Automation Technologies for Alert Triage

Organizations can leverage several automation technologies to enhance alert triage in SOCs:

Security Information and Event Management (SIEM) Systems

SIEM systems aggregate and analyze security data from various sources, generating alerts based on predefined rules. Modern SIEMs often incorporate machine learning capabilities to improve alert accuracy and reduce false positives. Automation within SIEMs can assist in alert categorization, prioritization, and even initial investigation.

Security Orchestration, Automation, and Response (SOAR)

SOAR platforms provide comprehensive automation capabilities for incident response. These platforms can integrate with existing security tools to automate the triage process, enforce playbooks, and initiate predefined response actions. SOAR solutions enable seamless collaboration between security tools, reducing manual intervention and accelerating incident response times.

Machine Learning and Artificial Intelligence

Machine learning algorithms can analyze historical alert data to identify patterns and improve triage accuracy. By learning from previous incidents, these algorithms can help distinguish between false positives and legitimate threats. AI-driven systems can also enhance threat detection capabilities, enabling proactive measures against emerging threats.

Threat Intelligence Platforms

Threat intelligence platforms provide real-time data on known threats, vulnerabilities, and attacker tactics. By integrating threat intelligence with automation tools, organizations can enhance alert triage by correlating alerts with existing threat data. This correlation allows SOC teams to prioritize alerts based on the current threat landscape.

Chatbots and Virtual Assistants

Chatbots can assist analysts in the triage process by answering common questions, providing guidance on incident response procedures, and even escalating alerts based on predefined criteria. These virtual assistants can improve operational efficiency by allowing analysts to focus on complex issues rather than routine inquiries.

Implementing Automated Alert Triage and Response in SOCs

To successfully implement automation in alert triage and response, organizations should follow a structured approach:

Assess Current Processes

Organizations should conduct a thorough assessment of their existing alert triage processes, identifying areas of inefficiency, high alert volumes, and common pain points experienced by analysts. This assessment will provide a baseline for implementing automation.

Define Automation Goals

Establish clear goals for automation, such as reducing alert response times, improving detection accuracy, or increasing the efficiency of SOC operations. Defining specific objectives will guide the selection of appropriate automation tools and strategies.

Select the Right Tools

Choose automation technologies that align with the organization's goals and existing security infrastructure. Consider the capabilities of SIEM, SOAR, and threat intelligence platforms, as well as the potential integration of machine learning algorithms.

Develop Automation Playbooks

Create detailed playbooks outlining the automation workflows for different types of alerts. These playbooks should include procedures for triage, escalation, and response actions, ensuring consistency in how alerts are handled.

Train SOC Analysts

Provide training for SOC analysts on using automation tools effectively. Analysts should understand how to interpret automated alerts, navigate the tools, and collaborate with automation to enhance their decision-making capabilities.

Monitor and Optimize Automation Performance

Continuously monitor the performance of automated alert triage and response processes. Collect feedback from SOC analysts to identify areas for improvement and refine automation workflows based on changing threat landscapes and organizational needs.

Benefits of Automating Alert Triage and Response in SOCs

Increased Efficiency

Automating alert triage frees up SOC analysts from repetitive tasks, allowing them to focus on more complex and high-priority incidents. This increased efficiency enhances the overall productivity of the SOC.

Improved Incident Response

With faster triage and response capabilities, organizations can mitigate threats more effectively. Rapid incident response minimizes the potential impact of cyberattacks, reducing the risk of data breaches and financial losses.

Enhanced Threat Detection

Automation can improve the accuracy of threat detection by applying consistent criteria for alert evaluation. This enhancement leads to better identification of legitimate threats, reducing the likelihood of overlooking critical incidents.

Scalability

As organizations grow and the volume of security alerts increases, automation allows SOCs to scale their operations without proportionally increasing personnel costs. Automated systems can handle larger volumes of alerts efficiently.

Data-Driven Insights

Automating alert triage enables organizations to collect and analyze data on alert patterns, response times, and analyst performance. These insights can inform future security strategies and help identify areas for further improvement.

Challenges of Automation in Alert Triage

False Positives and Negatives

While automation can reduce alert fatigue, it is not infallible. Poorly configured automation rules can lead to increased false positives or, conversely, missed legitimate threats. Continuous tuning and monitoring of automation tools are essential.

Complexity of Configuration

Implementing automation tools can be complex and requires careful configuration to ensure they align with the organization's security policies and workflows. Misconfiguration can hinder the effectiveness of automation efforts.

Resistance to Change

SOC analysts may resist automation efforts, fearing that their roles will be diminished. Organizations must communicate the benefits of automation clearly and emphasize that it enhances analysts' capabilities rather than replacing them.

Integration Challenges

Integrating automation tools with existing security infrastructure can be challenging, particularly in environments with diverse security products. Organizations should prioritize compatibility and integration during the selection process.

Skills Gap

Automating alert triage may require specialized skills in machine learning and data analysis. Organizations may need to invest in training or hire experts to effectively implement and manage automation solutions.

Automating alert triage and response in Security Operations Centers (SOCs) represents a transformative approach to managing the increasing volume and complexity of cybersecurity alerts. By leveraging automation technologies such as SIEM, SOAR, and machine learning, organizations can enhance the efficiency and effectiveness of their SOC operations.

Automation streamlines the triage process, reduces response times, and enables analysts to focus on higher-priority threats, ultimately improving overall cybersecurity posture. While challenges exist, including the risk of false positives and integration complexities, the benefits of automation far outweigh the drawbacks. Organizations that embrace automation in their SOCs will be better equipped to navigate the evolving threat landscape and respond to incidents proactively, ensuring the protection of critical assets and sensitive information. As the cyber threat landscape continues to evolve, automation will play an increasingly vital role in the future of cybersecurity operations.

7.2 AI-Assisted Threat Hunting: Enhancing Human Analysts' Capabilities

In the ever-evolving landscape of cybersecurity, proactive threat hunting has emerged as a critical component of a comprehensive defense strategy. Unlike traditional reactive measures that respond to alerts and incidents after they occur, threat hunting involves actively searching for hidden threats within an organization's network. This approach aims to identify and mitigate threats before they can inflict damage. As the sophistication of cyber threats increases, the complexity of the data that analysts must sift through also grows. This is where Artificial Intelligence (AI) comes into play, acting as a force multiplier that enhances human analysts' capabilities and effectiveness in threat hunting.

Understanding Threat Hunting

Threat hunting is the process of actively searching for indicators of compromise (IOCs) or abnormal behavior that traditional security measures may have overlooked. The objectives of threat hunting include:

Proactive Detection: Identifying threats that have already breached defenses but remain undetected by security systems.

Enhanced Visibility: Gaining a deeper understanding of network behavior and identifying anomalies that may indicate malicious activity.

Mitigation of Risks: Reducing the dwell time of threats within the environment by enabling quicker identification and remediation.

Improving Security Posture: Strengthening overall security strategies based on insights gained from hunting activities.

Effective threat hunting requires a combination of skilled human analysts and advanced technologies. The integration of AI into this process can significantly improve outcomes by augmenting human decision-making, streamlining data analysis, and enhancing the detection of advanced threats.

The Role of AI in Threat Hunting

AI technologies can assist threat hunters in several key areas:

Data Analysis and Correlation

AI algorithms can process vast amounts of data from various sources, including network logs, endpoint telemetry, and threat intelligence feeds. By correlating this data, AI can identify patterns and anomalies that may indicate malicious activity. Key capabilities include:

Anomaly Detection: AI can recognize deviations from normal behavior within network traffic, user activities, and system processes. By learning the baseline behaviors, AI can flag unusual activities that may signal an intrusion or breach.

Event Correlation: AI can analyze relationships between multiple events occurring across the network. For example, a series of failed login attempts followed by a successful login from an unusual location may indicate a potential compromise.

Machine Learning for Predictive Analytics

Machine learning (ML) algorithms can be trained on historical incident data to recognize indicators of future threats. By identifying patterns associated with previous attacks, ML can help threat hunters anticipate and identify emerging threats. This predictive capability allows for:

Threat Forecasting: ML can analyze trends in attack vectors and methods used by adversaries, helping organizations stay ahead of potential threats.

Behavioral Analytics: ML can track user and entity behavior over time, enabling the identification of unusual actions that deviate from established patterns.

Automated Investigative Processes

AI can automate many of the repetitive and time-consuming tasks associated with threat hunting. This includes:

Data Collection: AI can gather and normalize data from multiple sources, reducing the manual effort required by analysts.

Hypothesis Generation: AI can propose potential hypotheses for investigation based on observed anomalies, enabling analysts to focus on high-probability threats.

Initial Analysis: AI can conduct preliminary analyses of alerts and incidents, providing analysts with insights and recommendations for further investigation.

Natural Language Processing (NLP)

NLP techniques can enhance threat hunting by enabling analysts to search for and analyze textual data from various sources, such as threat reports, security blogs, and social media. This capability allows for:

Threat Intelligence Analysis: NLP can extract key entities and sentiments from unstructured data, helping analysts understand the context and relevance of emerging threats.

Knowledge Mining: Analysts can utilize NLP to uncover insights from vast amounts of documentation and past incident reports, identifying lessons learned that can inform future hunting activities.

Benefits of AI-Assisted Threat Hunting

Integrating AI into threat hunting offers several significant advantages:

Improved Efficiency

By automating data collection and preliminary analysis, AI allows human analysts to focus on more complex and critical tasks. This increased efficiency leads to quicker identification and response to threats.

Enhanced Accuracy

AI algorithms can analyze data more accurately than humans alone, reducing the likelihood of missed threats or false positives. The ability to correlate data across multiple dimensions enhances the overall effectiveness of threat detection.

Scalability

As organizations grow and the volume of data increases, AI-assisted threat hunting can scale to accommodate these changes. Automated systems can handle larger datasets without requiring proportional increases in personnel.

Continuous Learning

Machine learning models can continuously improve over time by learning from new data and threat landscapes. This adaptability ensures that threat hunting strategies remain relevant and effective against evolving threats.

Data-Driven Insights

AI can uncover trends and patterns that may not be immediately visible to human analysts. These insights can inform strategic decisions regarding security investments and risk management.

Challenges of AI-Assisted Threat Hunting

Despite its numerous benefits, the integration of AI into threat hunting also presents challenges:

False Positives and Negatives

While AI can enhance accuracy, it is not infallible. Poorly trained models may still produce false positives or miss legitimate threats. Ongoing tuning and validation of AI models are crucial.

Complexity of Implementation

Implementing AI solutions requires expertise in machine learning, data analysis, and cybersecurity. Organizations may face challenges in finding skilled personnel and integrating AI with existing systems.

Data Quality Issues

The effectiveness of AI algorithms depends on the quality and diversity of the training data. Incomplete or biased datasets can lead to inaccurate predictions and ineffective threat detection.

Ethical Considerations

The use of AI in threat hunting raises ethical concerns, particularly regarding privacy and surveillance. Organizations must ensure that their hunting practices comply with legal and ethical standards.

Dependence on Technology

Overreliance on AI can lead to complacency among human analysts. It is essential to maintain a balance between automated systems and human expertise, ensuring that analysts remain engaged and vigilant.

Best Practices for AI-Assisted Threat Hunting

To maximize the effectiveness of AI-assisted threat hunting, organizations should consider the following best practices:

Establish Clear Objectives

Define the goals of threat hunting initiatives, including specific outcomes and performance metrics. This clarity will guide the selection and implementation of AI tools.

Invest in Training and Skills Development

Provide ongoing training for security analysts to enhance their understanding of AI technologies and their role in threat hunting. Encourage collaboration between data scientists and security teams.

Focus on Data Quality

Ensure that the data used for training AI models is accurate, comprehensive, and representative of the organization's environment. Regularly update datasets to reflect changing threat landscapes.

Foster Collaboration Between Humans and AI

Emphasize the collaborative nature of AI-assisted threat hunting. Encourage analysts to work alongside AI systems, using the insights generated to inform their investigations and decision-making.

Monitor and Evaluate Performance

Continuously monitor the performance of AI models and threat hunting activities. Regular evaluations will identify areas for improvement and ensure that AI tools remain effective.

AI-assisted threat hunting represents a significant advancement in the field of cybersecurity, empowering human analysts to enhance their capabilities in identifying and mitigating threats. By leveraging AI for data analysis, predictive analytics, and automation, organizations can improve their proactive defense strategies and respond more effectively to emerging threats.

As the cybersecurity landscape continues to evolve, the integration of AI into threat hunting will be critical for staying ahead of sophisticated adversaries. While challenges exist, the benefits of AI-assisted threat hunting far outweigh the drawbacks, providing organizations with the tools needed to navigate the complexities of modern cybersecurity. Embracing AI in threat hunting is not just an enhancement of existing practices; it is a necessary evolution in the ongoing fight against cyber threats.

7.3 The Role of AI in SOC Workflow Optimization and Incident Prioritization

In the rapidly evolving landscape of cybersecurity, Security Operations Centers (SOCs) play a pivotal role in protecting organizations from a myriad of cyber threats. As cyberattacks become more sophisticated and frequent, SOC teams face unprecedented challenges, including high volumes of alerts, limited resources, and the need for rapid incident response. To address these challenges effectively, many organizations are turning to Artificial Intelligence (AI) as a transformative solution. AI technologies can optimize SOC workflows and enhance incident prioritization, allowing teams to respond more effectively to threats while maximizing their operational efficiency.

Understanding SOC Workflows and Incident Prioritization

A SOC's primary responsibilities include monitoring security events, detecting anomalies, investigating potential incidents, and responding to threats. The SOC workflow typically involves several key steps:

Alert Generation: Security tools and systems generate alerts based on predefined rules or anomaly detection.

Alert Triage: Analysts assess alerts to determine their severity and relevance. This step often involves categorizing alerts and prioritizing them for further investigation.

Investigation: Analysts conduct in-depth investigations of prioritized alerts to confirm whether they represent genuine threats.

Response: Once a threat is confirmed, the SOC team initiates response actions, which may involve containment, remediation, or escalation.

Post-Incident Review: After resolving an incident, teams conduct a review to analyze what occurred, identify lessons learned, and improve future response strategies.

Each step in this workflow is critical, but the sheer volume of alerts can overwhelm SOC analysts, leading to alert fatigue and potential oversights. This is where AI can play a transformative role.

AI-Driven Workflow Optimization

AI technologies can enhance each step of the SOC workflow, streamlining processes and improving overall efficiency:

Automated Alert Generation and Filtering

AI can enhance the alert generation process by analyzing data from various security sources to produce more relevant alerts. Additionally, AI can filter out false positives and noise, allowing analysts to focus on alerts that pose real threats. By employing machine learning algorithms, AI systems can learn from historical alert data to identify patterns that indicate whether an alert is likely to be valid or false.

Example: An AI system might use historical data to recognize that certain types of alerts are consistently false positives, allowing it to reduce those alerts in the future, thus improving the signal-to-noise ratio.

Enhanced Alert Triage and Prioritization

In traditional SOCs, alert triage is often a manual and time-consuming process. AI can automate this step by assessing alerts based on various factors, including:

- **Severity**: AI can assign a risk score to each alert based on the potential impact and likelihood of an attack.
- **Context**: Incorporating contextual information, such as asset criticality, user behavior, and historical incident data, enables AI to prioritize alerts that pose the most significant threats to the organization.
- **Threat Intelligence Integration**: AI systems can correlate alerts with external threat intelligence feeds to enhance their relevance and urgency.

By automating and optimizing the triage process, AI enables analysts to concentrate on high-priority incidents that require immediate attention, thus improving response times and reducing the risk of overlooking critical threats.

Proactive Threat Detection and Investigation

AI's predictive capabilities can be leveraged to identify potential threats before they manifest. By analyzing patterns of normal behavior, AI can detect anomalies that might indicate a breach or attempted attack.

Example: An AI system can continuously monitor user behavior and flag deviations from established norms, such as unusual access patterns or atypical login times, allowing analysts to investigate these anomalies proactively.

Furthermore, AI can assist in the investigation phase by providing analysts with insights derived from data analysis. It can quickly gather and analyze relevant data, correlate information across different systems, and present findings to analysts, facilitating more informed decision-making.

Automated Incident Response

Once a threat is confirmed, rapid response is crucial to minimizing damage. AI can automate certain response actions based on predefined playbooks, ensuring that appropriate measures are taken without delay. This can include actions such as:

- **Blocking IP addresses**: Automatically quarantining an affected system to prevent further damage.
- **Executing scripts**: Running scripts that patch vulnerabilities or remove malicious files.
- **Alerting stakeholders**: Notifying relevant team members or stakeholders about the incident and the actions taken.

By automating these processes, AI not only speeds up response times but also reduces the risk of human error, ensuring that incidents are managed consistently and efficiently.

Enhancing Incident Prioritization with AI

Incident prioritization is a critical aspect of SOC operations. With limited resources and time constraints, it is essential to focus efforts on incidents that pose the highest risk to the organization. AI enhances incident prioritization through:

Risk Scoring and Contextual Analysis

AI algorithms can analyze alerts and incidents using a variety of criteria, including:

- **Asset Value**: Assessing the importance of the affected asset to the organization's operations.
- **User Behavior**: Evaluating whether the actions of users are consistent with their roles and responsibilities.

- **Threat Intelligence Correlation**: Integrating external threat data to identify whether the incident is associated with known threats or vulnerabilities.

By scoring incidents based on these factors, AI can help SOC teams prioritize their responses effectively, ensuring that the most critical incidents are addressed first.

Machine Learning Models for Predictive Insights

AI can employ machine learning models trained on historical incident data to predict the likelihood of an incident evolving into a more severe attack. By identifying patterns associated with previous incidents, AI can help SOC teams focus their resources on incidents with a higher probability of escalation.

Example: If historical data shows that certain types of alerts frequently lead to data breaches, AI can flag similar incidents for immediate attention.
Dynamic Prioritization Based on Evolving Threats

The threat landscape is constantly changing, and new vulnerabilities and attack methods emerge regularly. AI systems can dynamically adjust prioritization based on real-time threat intelligence and emerging attack trends. This adaptability ensures that SOC teams are always focused on the most relevant threats, even as the environment evolves.

Benefits of AI-Driven SOC Optimization

The integration of AI into SOC workflows and incident prioritization offers numerous benefits:

Increased Efficiency and Productivity

By automating repetitive tasks and optimizing workflows, AI enables SOC analysts to concentrate on high-value activities, significantly enhancing productivity.

Improved Incident Response Times

Faster alert triage, investigation, and response result in reduced dwell times for threats, minimizing the potential impact of incidents.

Enhanced Accuracy and Reduced Fatigue

AI reduces the risk of alert fatigue by filtering out irrelevant alerts and improving the accuracy of threat detection. This leads to more informed decision-making and fewer missed threats.

Scalability

AI-driven systems can easily scale to handle increasing volumes of alerts and incidents without requiring proportional increases in personnel, making them well-suited for growing organizations.

Continuous Improvement

AI models can learn from new data and evolving threats, allowing organizations to adapt their security strategies continually.

Challenges and Considerations

While the benefits of AI in SOC optimization are significant, organizations should also be aware of potential challenges:

Quality of Data

The effectiveness of AI algorithms depends on the quality of the data used for training and analysis. Inaccurate or biased data can lead to erroneous conclusions and decisions.

Complexity of Implementation

Integrating AI technologies into existing SOC workflows requires careful planning and expertise. Organizations may face challenges in configuring AI tools to align with their specific needs and workflows.

Human Oversight

While AI can enhance SOC operations, human oversight remains crucial. Analysts must remain engaged in the decision-making process, leveraging AI insights while exercising their judgment and expertise.

Cost Considerations

Implementing AI solutions may involve significant initial investments in technology and training. Organizations should evaluate the potential return on investment and long-term benefits.

Ethical and Legal Implications

The use of AI in cybersecurity raises ethical considerations, particularly regarding privacy and surveillance. Organizations must ensure compliance with legal regulations and ethical standards.

AI plays a transformative role in optimizing SOC workflows and enhancing incident prioritization, empowering security teams to respond more effectively to cyber threats. By automating repetitive tasks, improving alert triage processes, and enabling proactive threat detection, AI significantly enhances the capabilities of SOC analysts.

As the threat landscape continues to evolve, integrating AI into SOC operations will be crucial for organizations seeking to strengthen their cybersecurity posture. By embracing AI-driven optimization, SOCs can not only improve their efficiency and response times but also stay ahead of sophisticated adversaries in the ongoing battle for cybersecurity. The future of SOC operations lies in the synergy between human expertise and AI capabilities, creating a resilient defense against the ever-increasing threats faced by organizations today.

Chapter 8: The Ethical Challenges of AI in Cybersecurity

In this chapter, we confront the ethical dilemmas and challenges that arise from the integration of artificial intelligence in cybersecurity. While AI offers significant advantages in threat detection and response, it also raises critical concerns regarding privacy, bias, and accountability. We explore how algorithmic bias can lead to unfair treatment of individuals or groups, affecting decision-making processes in areas such as user monitoring and threat assessments. Additionally, we delve into the ethical implications of surveillance technologies powered by AI, examining the delicate balance between ensuring security and protecting personal privacy. The chapter also discusses accountability in AI-driven systems: if an AI makes a decision that results in a data breach or wrongful accusation, who is responsible? Through case studies and expert opinions, we analyze these ethical challenges and propose best practices for developing responsible AI systems in cybersecurity. By fostering a thoughtful approach to the use of AI, organizations can harness its power while safeguarding fundamental ethical principles and maintaining public trust.

8.1 Algorithmic Bias: The Risks of Biased AI in Security

As organizations increasingly rely on Artificial Intelligence (AI) to enhance their cybersecurity measures, the implications of algorithmic bias have become a pressing concern. Algorithmic bias refers to the systematic and unfair discrimination that can occur when AI systems are trained on data that reflects existing inequalities or prejudices. In cybersecurity, biased AI can lead to serious consequences, including missed threats, wrongful accusations, and a failure to protect vulnerable populations. Understanding the nature of algorithmic bias, its potential impacts, and how to mitigate these risks is crucial for ensuring that AI systems enhance rather than undermine security efforts.

Understanding Algorithmic Bias

Algorithmic bias can arise from various sources, including:

Data Bias: AI systems learn from historical data, and if that data is skewed or unrepresentative, the AI model may inherit those biases. For example, if a dataset used to train a security system contains predominantly data from a specific demographic, the AI may fail to recognize threats associated with underrepresented groups.

Model Bias: The design of the algorithm itself can introduce bias. Certain algorithms may inherently favor specific types of data or decision-making processes, leading to unfair outcomes. For instance, a model that prioritizes speed over accuracy may overlook critical threats if they don't fit expected patterns.

Human Bias: The biases of developers and data scientists can also seep into AI systems. If individuals creating algorithms have preconceived notions or biases, these can manifest in the final AI outputs.

These biases can have significant implications in security contexts, where the stakes are high, and the consequences of error can be severe.

Potential Risks of Biased AI in Cybersecurity

False Negatives: Undetected Threats

Biased AI may fail to recognize certain types of threats, particularly those that do not conform to the patterns seen in the training data. For example, if an AI system is trained primarily on data from large enterprises, it may struggle to detect threats specific to small or medium-sized businesses, which often have different attack vectors and security challenges.

Example: A financial institution uses an AI system to monitor transactions for fraudulent activity. If the training data predominantly includes transactions from high-income users, the AI might fail to identify suspicious transactions from lower-income customers, leaving the institution vulnerable to fraud in that demographic.

False Positives: Misidentifying Innocent Behavior

Conversely, biased AI can lead to an increase in false positives, flagging legitimate behavior as malicious. This can result in unnecessary investigations, wasted resources, and diminished trust in the security systems.

Example: A security system trained on data that associates certain user behaviors with malicious activity may wrongfully flag employees from specific backgrounds or locations as potential threats, causing disruption and harming workplace morale.

Reinforcement of Existing Inequalities

If biased AI systems are implemented in security contexts, they can reinforce existing inequalities and vulnerabilities. For instance, if law enforcement agencies use biased AI tools to predict criminal behavior, marginalized communities may face increased scrutiny and over-policing based on flawed assumptions.

Example: AI-driven surveillance tools may disproportionately target specific neighborhoods, leading to more frequent monitoring of residents without a corresponding increase in actual criminal activity.

Erosion of Privacy and Trust

The use of biased AI can erode trust between organizations and the communities they serve. If people feel they are unfairly targeted or surveilled by biased systems, they may become less willing to engage with organizations, share information, or report suspicious activity.

Example: Users may be hesitant to use services that employ AI for monitoring if they believe their behavior is being misinterpreted, leading to a chilling effect on open communication and collaboration.

Regulatory and Legal Risks

Organizations that deploy biased AI systems may also face legal repercussions. Discriminatory outcomes can lead to lawsuits, regulatory scrutiny, and reputational damage.

Example: If a company uses an AI-driven security system that disproportionately targets a specific demographic, it may be subject to investigations for violating anti-discrimination laws.

Mitigating Algorithmic Bias in Security AI

Addressing algorithmic bias in AI systems requires a multifaceted approach:

Diverse and Representative Datasets

Organizations should prioritize the use of diverse datasets that accurately represent the populations and behaviors they intend to monitor. This involves collecting data from a broad range of sources and ensuring that no particular group is over- or under-represented.

Action Item: When creating training datasets, involve stakeholders from various demographics to ensure inclusivity and relevance.

Algorithm Transparency and Explainability

AI models should be transparent, allowing users to understand how decisions are made. Explainable AI (XAI) frameworks can help reveal the factors influencing AI outputs, making it easier to identify and address biases.

Action Item: Implement XAI techniques that allow security teams to understand why certain alerts are triggered, enabling them to adjust models accordingly.

Regular Auditing and Monitoring

Continuous evaluation of AI systems is essential to identify and rectify biases as they emerge. Regular audits can assess model performance, ensuring that it remains fair and effective over time.

Action Item: Establish a schedule for periodic audits of AI systems, focusing on performance metrics across different demographic groups.

Human Oversight

Maintaining human oversight in AI decision-making is crucial. Analysts should review AI-generated outputs to validate findings and ensure that biases do not lead to erroneous conclusions.

Action Item: Create a structured process for analysts to review flagged incidents and provide feedback on AI performance.

Incorporating Ethical Considerations

Organizations should embed ethical considerations into their AI development processes. Establishing ethical guidelines can help guide decision-making and ensure that the implementation of AI aligns with broader societal values.

Action Item: Develop an ethical framework for AI use in security, incorporating input from diverse stakeholders to ensure comprehensive perspectives.

Training and Awareness Programs

Educating employees about algorithmic bias and its implications is essential for fostering a culture of awareness and responsibility. Training programs can help staff understand the importance of addressing biases in AI systems.

Action Item: Conduct training sessions that cover the risks of algorithmic bias and the organization's commitment to fair AI practices.

Algorithmic bias presents significant risks in the realm of cybersecurity, potentially leading to false negatives, false positives, and the reinforcement of existing inequalities. As organizations increasingly rely on AI to enhance their security posture, it is crucial to address these biases to ensure that AI systems function fairly and effectively.

By prioritizing diverse data sources, promoting transparency, conducting regular audits, maintaining human oversight, and fostering an ethical approach, organizations can mitigate the risks associated with algorithmic bias. This proactive stance will not only enhance the effectiveness of AI in cybersecurity but also help build trust and accountability in the deployment of these powerful technologies. In an age where the stakes are high, ensuring fairness in AI is not just an ethical imperative but also a strategic necessity for successful cybersecurity initiatives.

8.2 Accountability in AI: Who is Responsible for Automated Decisions?

As Artificial Intelligence (AI) systems become integral to various sectors, including cybersecurity, the question of accountability for automated decisions looms large. The complexity of AI algorithms and their capacity for independent operation introduce challenges in establishing clear lines of responsibility. This chapter explores the intricacies of accountability in AI, examining who bears the responsibility for the actions taken by AI systems and the implications of these decisions in the context of cybersecurity.

Understanding Accountability in AI Systems

Accountability refers to the obligation to explain, justify, and take responsibility for one's actions. In the context of AI, this includes the decisions made by algorithms and the outcomes they produce. As AI systems are increasingly deployed to make critical decisions, such as identifying potential cyber threats or automating incident responses, the need for clear accountability becomes paramount.

The Challenge of Autonomy

AI systems, particularly those driven by machine learning, can operate with a degree of autonomy that complicates accountability. These systems learn from data, adapt over time, and make decisions based on algorithms that may not be fully understood even by their creators. This raises important questions:

Who is responsible when an AI system makes a mistake?

How do we attribute accountability when an algorithm's decision leads to negative consequences?
Decision-Making Spectrum

To better understand accountability, it's essential to consider the spectrum of AI decision-making:

- **Fully Automated Decisions**: In these cases, an AI system makes decisions without human intervention. For example, an AI-driven cybersecurity system that automatically blocks an IP address deemed suspicious operates autonomously.
- **Human-AI Collaboration**: In this model, AI provides recommendations based on data analysis, but human operators make the final decision. This could include an analyst reviewing AI-generated alerts before taking action.
- **Human-Only Decisions**: Traditional decision-making scenarios where humans analyze data and make decisions without AI assistance.

The degree of autonomy in AI systems directly influences accountability. In fully automated systems, it can be challenging to pinpoint responsibility when things go wrong.

The Key Stakeholders in AI Accountability

Establishing accountability in AI involves multiple stakeholders, each with roles and responsibilities:

Developers and Data Scientists

Those who design and train AI systems bear a degree of responsibility for the algorithms they create. They must ensure that the data used is representative and free from bias, and that the algorithms are transparent and understandable.

Accountability Implications: Developers must conduct thorough testing and validation to minimize errors and biases in AI outputs. If an AI system makes a faulty decision, developers may be held accountable for not adhering to best practices.

Organizations and Deployers

The organizations that deploy AI systems carry significant responsibility for how those systems are used. They must establish governance frameworks that outline accountability structures, ethical guidelines, and compliance with regulations.

Accountability Implications: If an AI system leads to a data breach or wrongful termination of access rights, the organization may face legal liability. This underscores the importance of due diligence in selecting, implementing, and monitoring AI technologies.

End Users and Human Oversight

Human operators who interact with AI systems play a crucial role in ensuring that automated decisions are appropriate. They are responsible for validating AI-generated outputs, especially in critical applications like cybersecurity.

Accountability Implications: If an operator blindly follows an AI recommendation without scrutiny and a mistake occurs, they may share in the accountability for the resulting consequences.

Regulators and Policymakers

Regulatory bodies are increasingly recognizing the need for frameworks that govern AI accountability. They play a vital role in setting standards, creating guidelines, and ensuring that organizations comply with ethical and legal obligations.

Accountability Implications: Failure to adhere to regulations can result in penalties for organizations, emphasizing the need for clear accountability mechanisms in AI deployment.

Society and the Public

Ultimately, society as a whole has a stake in the accountability of AI systems. Public perception of AI can be significantly influenced by how responsibly organizations manage and govern these technologies.

Accountability Implications: If AI systems are perceived as biased or harmful, public trust can erode, leading to calls for greater accountability and regulation in AI deployment.

Challenges in Establishing Accountability

Despite the clarity of the roles and responsibilities among stakeholders, several challenges complicate accountability in AI:

Black Box Nature of AI

Many AI algorithms, particularly deep learning models, function as "black boxes," making it difficult to understand how they arrive at specific decisions. This lack of transparency can hinder accountability, as stakeholders may struggle to justify or explain an AI's actions.

Implication: If an AI system blocks legitimate access due to a misinterpretation of data, organizations may find it challenging to explain the rationale behind that decision.

Complexity of Decision-Making Processes

AI systems often involve intricate decision-making processes influenced by various factors, making it challenging to trace the exact cause of an outcome. This complexity can obfuscate accountability.

Implication: When multiple data inputs and algorithms interact, determining which factor contributed to a negative outcome may be difficult, complicating efforts to hold parties accountable.

Legal and Regulatory Gaps

Many jurisdictions lack comprehensive legal frameworks governing AI accountability. As a result, organizations may face uncertainty about their legal responsibilities and liabilities when deploying AI systems.

Implication: The absence of clear regulations can lead to inconsistent practices, with organizations unsure of how to navigate accountability issues in AI.

Rapidly Evolving Technology

The pace of AI development often outstrips the ability of regulatory bodies to establish relevant frameworks. This lag can create challenges in ensuring that accountability measures are current and applicable.

Implication: Organizations may operate in a regulatory gray area, leading to uncertainty about their obligations and responsibilities.

Strategies for Enhancing Accountability in AI

To address the challenges of accountability in AI, organizations can adopt several strategies:

Develop Clear Governance Frameworks

Establishing governance structures that outline roles, responsibilities, and accountability mechanisms is crucial. This framework should include policies for transparency, ethics, and risk management.

Action Item: Organizations should create a dedicated team to oversee AI governance, ensuring that accountability measures are integrated into all stages of AI development and deployment.

Promote Explainability and Transparency

Investing in explainable AI (XAI) initiatives can help organizations demystify AI decision-making processes. Transparent systems enable stakeholders to understand how decisions are made and to hold the responsible parties accountable.

Action Item: Implement AI models that provide clear explanations for their outputs, allowing users to understand the rationale behind decisions.

Conduct Regular Audits and Assessments

Periodic audits of AI systems can help organizations evaluate performance, identify biases, and ensure compliance with established governance frameworks. Auditing can enhance accountability by providing insights into AI behavior and decision-making.

Action Item: Establish a schedule for regular audits of AI systems, focusing on transparency, bias detection, and compliance with ethical standards.

Foster a Culture of Accountability

Encouraging a culture of accountability within organizations is essential. Employees should be trained to understand their roles in ensuring that AI systems are used responsibly and ethically.

Action Item: Develop training programs that emphasize accountability in AI, including case studies and best practices for ethical AI deployment.

Engage with Stakeholders

Organizations should engage with diverse stakeholders, including policymakers, industry leaders, and affected communities, to develop comprehensive accountability frameworks. Collaborative approaches can lead to more effective governance and better outcomes for all.

Action Item: Establish forums for dialogue between organizations and stakeholders to discuss accountability issues, share experiences, and identify solutions.

As AI systems become increasingly integrated into cybersecurity and other sectors, the question of accountability for automated decisions becomes more pressing. Establishing clear lines of responsibility among developers, organizations, end users, regulators, and society is essential for ensuring that AI operates ethically and effectively.

By addressing the challenges of algorithmic bias, transparency, and the complexity of decision-making processes, organizations can enhance accountability in their AI systems. Through the development of governance frameworks, promotion of explainability, regular audits, and stakeholder engagement, they can foster a culture of responsibility that ultimately strengthens trust in AI technologies.

In an era where AI plays a pivotal role in shaping our security landscape, establishing accountability is not merely a regulatory necessity but a moral imperative. As we navigate the complexities of automated decisions, prioritizing accountability will ensure that AI contributes positively to our society, enhancing cybersecurity while safeguarding individual rights and freedoms.

8.3 Balancing Privacy and Security: AI's Ethical Implications

The integration of Artificial Intelligence (AI) into cybersecurity presents a dual-edged sword: while it offers significant enhancements in threat detection and response, it also raises profound ethical questions surrounding privacy and individual rights. As organizations leverage AI technologies to monitor, analyze, and respond to potential security threats, the balance between ensuring security and respecting privacy becomes increasingly precarious. This chapter delves into the ethical implications of using AI in cybersecurity, examining the challenges of balancing privacy and security, and proposing strategies to navigate this complex landscape.

Understanding the Privacy-Security Dichotomy

Privacy Defined

Privacy refers to the right of individuals to control their personal information and how it is collected, used, and shared. In the digital age, where vast amounts of data are generated daily, ensuring privacy becomes critical, as breaches can lead to identity theft, financial loss, and a loss of trust in organizations.

Example: Social media platforms collect extensive user data for targeted advertising, raising concerns about user privacy and consent.

Security Defined

Security, particularly in the context of cybersecurity, refers to the protection of information systems from unauthorized access, damage, or disruption. Organizations deploy various measures, including AI-driven technologies, to identify and mitigate threats, ensuring the integrity and confidentiality of data.

Example: Organizations use AI to analyze network traffic for signs of intrusions, potentially compromising individual privacy in the process.

The Ethical Dilemma

The ethical dilemma arises when the measures taken to enhance security encroach upon individual privacy rights. AI systems capable of analyzing large datasets for patterns may inadvertently infringe on personal privacy if not managed carefully.

Example: Surveillance systems utilizing facial recognition technology can enhance security but also raise concerns about mass surveillance and the erosion of civil liberties.

Challenges in Balancing Privacy and Security

Data Collection Practices

AI systems rely on extensive data collection to function effectively. However, the methods used to gather data can vary significantly in terms of ethical implications. Collecting data without informed consent or transparency can violate individuals' privacy rights.

Challenge: Organizations must navigate the fine line between gathering enough data for security purposes and respecting users' rights to privacy.

Potential for Surveillance

The deployment of AI in cybersecurity often entails monitoring user behavior, which can lead to invasive surveillance practices. While the intention may be to prevent security threats, such surveillance can create a chilling effect, discouraging open communication and free expression.

Challenge: Ensuring that monitoring practices are proportional and transparent is essential to avoid infringing on civil liberties.

Bias and Discrimination

AI systems can perpetuate biases present in the data they are trained on, leading to discriminatory practices that impact specific demographic groups. For example, if an AI system disproportionately flags certain ethnic groups as suspicious based on biased training data, it raises ethical concerns about fairness and equality.

Challenge: Organizations must be vigilant in ensuring that AI systems do not reinforce existing biases and that their use promotes equitable security practices.

Lack of Regulation and Oversight

The rapid advancement of AI technologies often outpaces the development of regulatory frameworks that govern their use. Without clear guidelines and oversight, organizations may engage in practices that compromise privacy without accountability.

Challenge: Establishing regulatory frameworks that address the ethical use of AI in cybersecurity is essential for protecting individual rights.

Strategies for Balancing Privacy and Security

Data Minimization

Organizations should adopt a principle of data minimization, collecting only the data necessary for achieving specific security objectives. This approach reduces the risk of privacy infringements and helps maintain compliance with data protection regulations.

Action Item: Conduct data audits to identify and eliminate unnecessary data collection practices, focusing on obtaining consent where applicable.

Transparent Data Practices

Transparency is crucial for building trust with users. Organizations should clearly communicate their data collection practices, how data will be used, and the measures in place to protect individual privacy.

Action Item: Develop clear privacy policies and user agreements that outline data usage and security practices in accessible language.

Implementing Ethical AI Frameworks

Organizations should develop ethical AI frameworks that guide the responsible use of AI technologies. These frameworks should address issues such as bias, discrimination, and the need for human oversight in automated decisions.

Action Item: Establish an ethical review board to assess AI projects and ensure compliance with established ethical standards.

Anonymization and Data Protection Techniques

Employing techniques such as data anonymization can mitigate privacy risks while still allowing organizations to benefit from AI-driven insights. By removing personally identifiable information (PII), organizations can analyze data without compromising individual privacy.

Action Item: Implement data anonymization techniques in AI training datasets to protect user identities while enabling effective analysis.

User Empowerment and Control

Empowering users to control their data enhances privacy while maintaining security. Providing individuals with options to opt in or out of data collection and giving them access to their data can build trust.

Action Item: Create user interfaces that allow individuals to manage their data preferences, including opting out of specific data collection practices.

Robust Regulatory Compliance

Organizations must stay informed about data protection regulations and ensure compliance with laws such as the General Data Protection Regulation (GDPR) and the California Consumer Privacy Act (CCPA). Adhering to these regulations fosters accountability and protects individual privacy.

Action Item: Conduct regular training sessions for employees on data protection regulations and their implications for AI practices.

The Role of Public Discourse and Policy

Engaging Stakeholders

Public discourse around AI, privacy, and security is vital for developing balanced policies. Engaging stakeholders, including industry experts, ethicists, and civil rights organizations, can foster dialogue and collaboration in creating responsible AI practices.

Action Item: Host public forums and discussions to explore the ethical implications of AI in cybersecurity and gather input from diverse perspectives.

Advocating for Comprehensive Policies

Policymakers must advocate for comprehensive regulations that balance the needs of security with the protection of individual privacy. This includes establishing standards for data collection, usage, and accountability in AI technologies.

Action Item: Collaborate with regulatory bodies to contribute to the development of policies that address the ethical use of AI in cybersecurity.

Balancing privacy and security in the context of AI-driven cybersecurity is a complex ethical challenge that requires careful consideration and proactive measures. As organizations deploy AI technologies to enhance security, they must remain vigilant in protecting individual privacy rights and addressing the ethical implications of their practices.

By adopting principles of data minimization, transparency, and user empowerment, organizations can create a framework that respects privacy while effectively managing security risks. Engaging in public discourse and advocating for comprehensive policies further ensures that AI is used responsibly, fostering a security landscape that is both effective and ethical.

In an era where the stakes are high, prioritizing privacy alongside security will not only enhance the effectiveness of AI in cybersecurity but also build trust and accountability in the deployment of these powerful technologies. As we navigate the complexities of this evolving landscape, a commitment to ethical principles will be essential for ensuring that AI serves the greater good while safeguarding individual rights.

Chapter 9: Adversarial AI: When AI is Weaponized

In this chapter, we delve into the darker side of artificial intelligence: its potential to be weaponized by cybercriminals and malicious actors. As AI technologies advance, so too do the methods used to exploit them. We explore the concept of adversarial machine learning, where attackers manipulate AI models by introducing subtle changes to the input data, causing these systems to misclassify or misinterpret threats. This chapter discusses various forms of AI-driven attacks, including AI-powered malware that can adapt and evade detection and deepfake technologies that can be used for social engineering and misinformation campaigns. Additionally, we examine the implications of adversarial AI for cybersecurity defenses, highlighting the need for robust countermeasures to safeguard against these sophisticated threats. By understanding how adversarial AI operates, organizations can better prepare themselves to defend against the evolving landscape of cyber threats, ensuring that their security measures remain effective in the face of rapidly changing technologies.

9.1 Adversarial Machine Learning: Manipulating AI Models

As the reliance on artificial intelligence (AI) grows, so does the understanding that AI systems are not infallible. One of the most pressing concerns is adversarial machine learning, a subfield focused on the strategies and techniques used to manipulate AI models through malicious inputs. Adversarial machine learning highlights the vulnerabilities inherent in AI systems, especially in applications like cybersecurity, where an attacker can exploit weaknesses to compromise the integrity of AI-driven defenses. This chapter explores the concept of adversarial machine learning, the techniques employed by adversaries, and the implications for cybersecurity.

Understanding Adversarial Machine Learning

Definition and Concept

Adversarial machine learning involves crafting inputs designed to deceive AI models into making incorrect predictions or classifications. These inputs, known as adversarial examples, are often imperceptible to human observers but can significantly disrupt an AI system's performance.

Example: A small perturbation to a digital image, undetectable by the human eye, can lead an image recognition system to misclassify it, such as identifying a stop sign as a yield sign.

The AI Vulnerability Landscape

AI models, particularly deep learning systems, are inherently complex and trained on vast amounts of data. This complexity, while beneficial for learning intricate patterns, also creates vulnerabilities. Adversaries can exploit these weaknesses by injecting adversarial examples, resulting in misclassifications and erroneous outputs.

Implication: The very features that make AI powerful—such as their ability to generalize from training data—also expose them to vulnerabilities that can be exploited by adversaries.

Techniques Used in Adversarial Machine Learning

Gradient-Based Attacks

One of the most common methods for generating adversarial examples is through gradient-based attacks, which leverage the gradients of the loss function to identify how small perturbations to input data can lead to significant changes in the output.

Example: The Fast Gradient Sign Method (FGSM) computes the gradient of the loss concerning the input data and adjusts the input in the direction that maximally increases the loss, creating an adversarial example that is likely to be misclassified.

Optimization-Based Attacks

These attacks utilize optimization techniques to find the smallest perturbation needed to change the AI model's output. By minimizing the difference between the original input and the adversarial input while maximizing the probability of a misclassification, attackers can create highly effective adversarial examples.

Example: The Carlini & Wagner (C&W) attack optimizes perturbations to create examples that are difficult to detect while ensuring they successfully deceive the model.

Transferability Attacks

An interesting property of adversarial examples is their transferability. Adversarial examples crafted to deceive one model can often mislead other models trained on different datasets. This feature arises from shared vulnerabilities in AI architectures, enabling adversaries to craft a single adversarial example that can exploit multiple systems.

Example: An adversary might train an adversarial example against a specific image recognition system, and that same example could successfully mislead a different model trained with a distinct approach, posing a significant threat to security systems using various AI models.

Implications of Adversarial Machine Learning for Cybersecurity

Threat to AI-Driven Security Systems

As organizations increasingly employ AI-driven security solutions, adversarial machine learning poses a significant threat. Attackers can craft adversarial examples specifically targeting these systems to bypass defenses, leading to undetected intrusions or false alarms.

Example: An adversary might modify network traffic patterns slightly, evading intrusion detection systems (IDS) that rely on AI for anomaly detection, thus gaining unauthorized access without triggering alerts.

Decreased Trust in AI Technologies

The existence of adversarial examples can undermine trust in AI technologies. If organizations are aware of the potential for adversarial manipulation, they may become hesitant to deploy AI-driven solutions, fearing vulnerabilities could be exploited.

Implication: To maintain confidence in AI systems, developers must address these vulnerabilities through robust defenses and transparent communication regarding AI limitations.

Need for Robustness and Resilience

The emergence of adversarial machine learning necessitates a shift in how AI models are designed and deployed. There is an increasing emphasis on creating models that are resilient to adversarial attacks, incorporating mechanisms to detect and mitigate such threats.

Action Item: Organizations must invest in adversarial training, which involves exposing models to adversarial examples during training to improve their robustness and reduce susceptibility to future attacks.

Strategies for Mitigating Adversarial Attacks

Adversarial Training

One effective approach to enhancing model robustness is adversarial training, which involves training the AI model on a mixture of original and adversarial examples. This technique allows the model to learn to recognize and appropriately respond to adversarial inputs, improving its resilience.

Implementation: Organizations can integrate adversarial examples into their training datasets, allowing models to learn how to identify and mitigate the impact of such attacks.

Input Preprocessing Techniques

Preprocessing inputs before they are fed into the model can help filter out adversarial examples. Techniques such as input transformation or feature squeezing can reduce the effectiveness of adversarial attacks by simplifying the input data.

Implementation: Organizations can implement preprocessing pipelines that modify inputs (e.g., reducing resolution, applying noise) to minimize the potential for adversarial manipulation.

Model Ensembling

Utilizing multiple models to make predictions can enhance robustness against adversarial attacks. By averaging predictions from different models, organizations can reduce the likelihood of being misled by adversarial examples targeted at a single model.

Implementation: Deploying an ensemble of diverse models allows organizations to leverage the strengths of different architectures and reduce susceptibility to specific attack vectors.

Detection Mechanisms

Developing mechanisms to detect adversarial examples is essential for safeguarding AI systems. These detection methods can involve analyzing input data for irregularities or patterns indicative of adversarial manipulation.

Implementation: Organizations can deploy anomaly detection systems that monitor input data streams for signs of adversarial examples and trigger alerts or countermeasures when detected.

Adversarial machine learning represents a significant challenge in the evolving landscape of AI and cybersecurity. As AI systems become increasingly integral to security infrastructures, the potential for adversarial manipulation raises urgent questions about their reliability and resilience.

Understanding the techniques employed in adversarial machine learning, as well as the implications for cybersecurity, is essential for organizations aiming to protect their systems against these threats. By investing in robust defenses, including adversarial training, input preprocessing, model ensembling, and detection mechanisms, organizations can enhance the security of their AI-driven systems.

In an era where AI is at the forefront of cybersecurity solutions, addressing the vulnerabilities associated with adversarial machine learning is not merely a technical challenge but a strategic imperative. By proactively mitigating these risks, organizations can ensure that their AI systems remain effective defenders against an increasingly sophisticated landscape of cyber threats.

9.2 AI-Powered Malware and Ransomware: A New Generation of Cyber Threats

As cyber threats continue to evolve, the integration of artificial intelligence (AI) into malware and ransomware has given rise to a new generation of cyber threats that are more sophisticated, adaptive, and challenging to detect. AI-powered malware leverages machine learning and advanced algorithms to enhance its capabilities, allowing it to evade traditional cybersecurity measures and increase its effectiveness in carrying out attacks. This chapter delves into the characteristics of AI-powered malware and ransomware, their implications for cybersecurity, and strategies to defend against these advanced threats.

Understanding AI-Powered Malware and Ransomware

Definition and Characteristics

AI-powered malware refers to malicious software that utilizes AI algorithms to improve its ability to infect systems, spread autonomously, and adapt to countermeasures. This class of malware can analyze its environment, learn from interactions, and optimize its behavior to increase the chances of successful infiltration and persistence.

Example: An AI-powered trojan could modify its payload based on the security software detected on a target machine, rendering itself invisible to conventional detection methods.

Ransomware, a specific type of malware, encrypts a victim's files and demands a ransom for the decryption key. The integration of AI enhances ransomware capabilities by allowing it to target specific files, optimize the encryption process, and determine the best times to strike for maximum impact.

Example: An AI-driven ransomware variant may analyze a user's activity patterns to identify when to launch its attack, increasing the likelihood that the victim will pay the ransom.

Evolution of Malware and Ransomware

Traditionally, malware relied on static techniques and predefined signatures to execute attacks. However, the advent of AI has transformed malware development and deployment. By leveraging machine learning models, cybercriminals can create malware that learns from its environment, making it more resilient to detection and response efforts.

Implication: The shift towards AI-powered malware marks a significant evolution in cyber threats, as attackers are now able to develop more complex and adaptive strategies.

Techniques Employed in AI-Powered Malware

Behavioral Analysis

AI algorithms enable malware to analyze the behavior of both users and systems. By understanding normal operational patterns, AI-powered malware can blend in with legitimate activities, avoiding detection by traditional security solutions that rely on signature-based detection.

Example: An AI-driven backdoor may monitor user behavior to avoid triggering alerts, waiting for the opportune moment to execute malicious commands without raising suspicion.

Self-Learning Capabilities

One of the most significant advancements in AI-powered malware is its ability to learn and adapt over time. Through reinforcement learning, these malicious programs can refine their strategies based on feedback from their interactions with targeted systems.

Example: A piece of AI malware might learn which types of file encryption are most effective against a particular operating system, adjusting its approach accordingly to maximize impact.

Automated Attack Optimization

AI-powered malware can automate the process of testing various attack vectors, identifying weaknesses in security defenses, and optimizing its approach to increase the chances of success.

Example: By employing genetic algorithms, malware can mutate its code to find the most effective variant that evades detection while still fulfilling its malicious objectives. Implications for Cybersecurity.

Increased Sophistication of Attacks

The rise of AI-powered malware means that cybercriminals can orchestrate more sophisticated attacks that are harder to detect and defend against. Traditional cybersecurity measures may struggle to keep pace with these evolving threats, resulting in heightened risk for organizations.

Implication: Organizations must continuously update and improve their cybersecurity strategies to defend against increasingly complex malware variants.

Greater Potential for Automation in Cyber Attacks

AI technologies facilitate the automation of cyber attacks, allowing criminals to launch attacks at scale without human intervention. This capability can lead to widespread damage in a short amount of time, overwhelming traditional security resources.

Example: Automated attacks leveraging AI can initiate large-scale phishing campaigns, compromising numerous accounts before defenders can respond.

Evolving Ransomware Tactics

The integration of AI into ransomware tactics enables attackers to customize their approach based on the target. By analyzing the target's data and vulnerabilities, AI-driven ransomware can optimize its encryption methods, ensuring that it maximizes its chances of extracting a ransom.

Example: An AI-driven ransomware variant might selectively encrypt only the most critical files of an organization, applying pressure for a quick ransom payment.

Defensive Strategies Against AI-Powered Malware and Ransomware

Adopting Advanced Threat Detection Solutions

Organizations must invest in advanced threat detection solutions that utilize AI and machine learning to identify anomalous behavior indicative of AI-powered malware. These solutions can analyze vast amounts of data in real time, enabling faster detection of emerging threats.

Action Item: Implement behavior-based detection systems that monitor network traffic and system activities for signs of unusual or malicious behavior.

Threat Intelligence Sharing

Collaborating with industry peers and participating in threat intelligence sharing initiatives can enhance an organization's ability to stay informed about emerging AI-driven threats. Sharing insights about new malware variants and attack techniques can help organizations improve their defenses.

Action Item: Join threat intelligence networks to access shared information about AI-powered malware and ransomware attacks.

Continuous Training and Awareness Programs

Human error remains one of the most significant vulnerabilities in cybersecurity. Organizations should prioritize ongoing training and awareness programs to educate employees about the risks posed by AI-powered threats, emphasizing the importance of recognizing suspicious behavior and potential phishing attempts.

Action Item: Develop training modules that specifically address the characteristics and tactics of AI-powered malware and ransomware, equipping employees with the knowledge to identify potential threats.

Implementing Incident Response Plans

Organizations should have robust incident response plans in place to address potential AI-powered malware and ransomware incidents. These plans should include predefined protocols for identifying, containing, and mitigating threats quickly and effectively.

Action Item: Regularly test and update incident response plans to ensure that they are equipped to handle emerging AI-driven threats.

Enhancing Endpoint Security Measures

Given that many AI-powered attacks target endpoints, organizations must implement robust endpoint security measures. This includes deploying advanced endpoint detection and response (EDR) solutions that utilize AI for proactive threat hunting and response.

Action Item: Invest in EDR solutions that can identify and respond to suspicious activities on endpoints in real time.

AI-powered malware and ransomware represent a new frontier in the landscape of cyber threats, characterized by increased sophistication and adaptability. As cybercriminals continue to leverage AI technologies to enhance their malicious capabilities, organizations must remain vigilant and proactive in their defense strategies.

Understanding the nature of AI-powered malware and ransomware is essential for developing effective responses to these threats. By investing in advanced detection solutions, fostering collaboration through threat intelligence sharing, and prioritizing employee training, organizations can enhance their resilience against the growing wave of AI-driven cyber threats.

As the battle between defenders and attackers intensifies, embracing innovative strategies and technologies will be crucial for navigating the evolving cybersecurity landscape. By staying informed and prepared, organizations can safeguard their systems and data against the sophisticated tactics employed by AI-powered malware and ransomware, ensuring a more secure digital future.

9.3 Defending Against AI-Driven Attacks: Strategies for Resilience

As artificial intelligence (AI) continues to reshape the landscape of cybersecurity, it brings both opportunities and challenges. On one hand, AI technologies can enhance defenses; on the other hand, they can be weaponized by malicious actors to orchestrate increasingly sophisticated attacks. The rise of AI-driven attacks necessitates a strategic approach to defense, focused on building resilience within organizations. This chapter explores effective strategies to defend against AI-driven attacks, emphasizing proactive measures, continuous adaptation, and a holistic cybersecurity posture.

Understanding AI-Driven Attacks

Characteristics of AI-Driven Attacks

AI-driven attacks are marked by their ability to learn, adapt, and evolve. They often utilize techniques such as:

- **Automation**: AI enables attackers to automate various aspects of their operations, from reconnaissance to exploitation, allowing for rapid and large-scale attacks.
- **Adaptive Techniques**: These attacks can adapt their tactics based on the defenses encountered, making them harder to predict and mitigate.
- **Impersonation and Deception**: Using natural language processing (NLP) and machine learning, attackers can create convincing phishing emails or impersonate legitimate users to bypass security measures.

Common Types of AI-Driven Attacks

- **Phishing and Social Engineering**: AI-generated phishing emails can be more convincing, as they can mimic the writing styles of trusted individuals or organizations.
- **Malware and Ransomware**: AI can be used to create advanced malware capable of evading detection and launching highly targeted attacks.
- **Data Exfiltration**: AI can optimize the methods for extracting sensitive data from compromised systems, making it easier for attackers to achieve their goals.

Strategies for Defending Against AI-Driven Attacks

Implementing Advanced Threat Detection Systems

To defend against AI-driven attacks, organizations must adopt advanced threat detection systems that utilize machine learning and AI for real-time monitoring and analysis. These systems can identify anomalies indicative of malicious activity, enabling faster response times.

Action Item: Invest in machine learning-based security solutions that can analyze user behavior, network traffic, and system activities to detect potential threats before they escalate.

Developing a Proactive Cyber Defense Framework

A proactive approach to cybersecurity is essential for defending against AI-driven attacks. This involves continuously assessing and updating security measures to stay ahead of emerging threats.

Action Item: Establish a framework for regular security assessments, vulnerability testing, and red teaming exercises to identify weaknesses in the security posture and remediate them proactively.

Enhancing Endpoint Security Measures

Given that many AI-driven attacks target endpoints, organizations must prioritize robust endpoint security. This includes deploying advanced endpoint detection and response (EDR) solutions that leverage AI to monitor and respond to suspicious activities in real time.

Action Item: Implement EDR solutions that provide real-time visibility into endpoint behavior, enabling rapid identification and remediation of threats.

Fostering a Security-First Culture

Human factors play a critical role in cybersecurity. Organizations should prioritize training and awareness programs that educate employees about the risks associated with AI-driven attacks, emphasizing the importance of vigilance and reporting suspicious activity.

Action Item: Develop comprehensive training programs that cover the characteristics of AI-driven threats and empower employees to recognize and respond to potential security incidents.

Leveraging Threat Intelligence Sharing

Collaborating with industry peers and participating in threat intelligence sharing initiatives can enhance an organization's ability to defend against AI-driven attacks. Sharing insights about new attack techniques and indicators of compromise can strengthen defenses across the community.

Action Item: Join threat intelligence networks to access shared information about AI-driven threats and contribute to collective defense efforts.

Investing in Automated Response Solutions

Automated response solutions can help organizations respond swiftly to AI-driven attacks, minimizing the potential damage. These solutions can analyze incidents, determine appropriate responses, and execute actions without human intervention.

Action Item: Implement security orchestration, automation, and response (SOAR) solutions to streamline incident response processes and reduce response times.

Adopting a Zero Trust Security Model

The Zero Trust security model operates on the principle of "never trust, always verify." By implementing a Zero Trust architecture, organizations can limit access to sensitive resources and require continuous verification of user identities, significantly reducing the risk of AI-driven attacks.

Action Item: Transition to a Zero Trust model by implementing identity and access management (IAM) solutions that enforce strict access controls and continuous authentication.

Conducting Regular Penetration Testing and Simulations

Regular penetration testing and simulations can help organizations identify vulnerabilities in their defenses and improve their incident response capabilities. By simulating AI-driven attacks, organizations can better understand their weaknesses and develop more effective strategies for resilience.

Action Item: Schedule routine penetration tests and red team exercises that focus on AI-driven attack vectors, enabling the organization to strengthen its defenses based on real-world scenarios.

Building Resilience Through Redundancy

Establishing redundancy in critical systems and data can enhance resilience against AI-driven attacks. By creating backups and ensuring that systems can quickly recover from attacks, organizations can minimize downtime and data loss.

Action Item: Implement robust backup and disaster recovery solutions to ensure that data can be restored quickly in the event of an attack.

Continuous Monitoring and Incident Response

Continuous monitoring of networks, systems, and user behavior is crucial for detecting AI-driven attacks in their early stages. Coupled with an effective incident response plan, continuous monitoring can significantly reduce the impact of attacks.

Action Item: Establish a Security Operations Center (SOC) that monitors for unusual activity 24/7 and can quickly respond to incidents, ensuring rapid containment and remediation of threats.

Defending against AI-driven attacks requires a multifaceted approach that combines advanced technologies, proactive strategies, and a strong organizational culture of security awareness. As cyber threats continue to evolve, organizations must be prepared to adapt their defenses to stay ahead of malicious actors leveraging AI.

By implementing advanced threat detection systems, fostering a security-first culture, and adopting a proactive cybersecurity framework, organizations can enhance their resilience against AI-driven attacks. Investing in continuous monitoring, automated response solutions, and threat intelligence sharing will further strengthen defenses in an increasingly complex cybersecurity landscape.

In this era of AI-driven cyber threats, resilience is paramount. Organizations that prioritize proactive measures and continuously adapt their security strategies will be better positioned to navigate the challenges posed by evolving AI technologies. By staying vigilant and prepared, organizations can protect their assets and ensure a secure digital future.

Chapter 10: AI in Cloud and IoT Security

In this chapter, we explore the transformative role of artificial intelligence in securing cloud environments and the Internet of Things (IoT). As organizations increasingly migrate their operations to the cloud and deploy interconnected devices, the attack surface expands, leading to new vulnerabilities and risks. We begin by discussing how AI enhances cloud security through advanced threat detection, automated compliance monitoring, and intelligent access management, ensuring that sensitive data is protected against unauthorized access and breaches. Next, we turn our attention to the unique challenges posed by IoT devices, which often lack robust security measures. We examine how AI can analyze data from these devices in real-time to identify anomalies and potential threats, enabling proactive defense strategies. Additionally, this chapter addresses the importance of implementing AI-driven security solutions that can adapt to the dynamic nature of cloud and IoT environments, offering organizations the resilience needed to safeguard their assets. By harnessing the power of AI, businesses can build a more secure foundation in an increasingly interconnected world.

10.1 Securing Cloud Infrastructures with AI

The rapid adoption of cloud computing has transformed the way organizations store, manage, and access data and applications. As more businesses migrate to cloud environments, the need for robust security measures has never been more critical. Cloud infrastructures are particularly attractive to cybercriminals due to their complexity and the vast amounts of sensitive data they handle. To counter these threats, organizations are increasingly turning to artificial intelligence (AI) to enhance cloud security. This chapter explores how AI can be leveraged to secure cloud infrastructures, the challenges associated with cloud security, and best practices for implementing AI-driven security measures.

Understanding Cloud Security Challenges

Complexity of Cloud Environments

Cloud environments often consist of multiple services and configurations, which can create security vulnerabilities if not managed correctly. The shared responsibility model of cloud security means that while cloud service providers (CSPs) secure the infrastructure, organizations must secure their data, applications, and configurations.

Implication: Misconfigurations, such as overly permissive access controls, can lead to data breaches and unauthorized access.

Increased Attack Surface

As organizations deploy more applications and services in the cloud, the attack surface expands, providing more opportunities for cybercriminals to exploit vulnerabilities. This increase in potential entry points complicates threat detection and incident response.

Example: An organization may deploy multiple cloud services, each with its own security controls, making it difficult to maintain consistent security policies across the entire infrastructure.

Data Privacy and Compliance Concerns

Storing sensitive data in the cloud raises concerns about data privacy and compliance with regulations such as GDPR, HIPAA, and others. Organizations must ensure that their cloud security measures align with these regulations to avoid penalties.

Challenge: Ensuring that data is encrypted and access controls are strictly enforced is crucial to maintaining compliance.

Insider Threats

Insider threats, whether malicious or accidental, pose significant risks to cloud security. Employees with access to sensitive data may inadvertently expose it or intentionally misuse their access.

Consideration: Organizations must implement measures to monitor user activity and detect anomalous behavior that may indicate insider threats.

The Role of AI in Cloud Security

AI-Powered Threat Detection

AI and machine learning algorithms can analyze vast amounts of data from cloud environments to identify unusual patterns and detect potential threats in real time. These systems can learn from historical data and adapt to new threats, enhancing their ability to identify anomalies that traditional security measures might miss.

Example: An AI-driven security information and event management (SIEM) solution can analyze logs and alerts from various cloud services to identify suspicious activities indicative of a breach.

Automated Response and Mitigation

AI can facilitate automated response mechanisms that enable organizations to respond to threats quickly and effectively. By analyzing data in real time, AI systems can initiate predefined response actions, such as isolating compromised resources or blocking malicious IP addresses.

Benefit: Automated responses can significantly reduce the time it takes to contain threats, minimizing potential damage.

Behavioral Analytics for User Activity Monitoring

AI-driven behavioral analytics can monitor user activities in cloud environments to identify deviations from normal behavior. By establishing baselines for user behavior, these systems can detect insider threats, compromised accounts, and other suspicious activities.

Example: If a user typically accesses cloud resources during business hours but suddenly attempts to access sensitive data at odd hours, an AI system can flag this behavior for further investigation.

Vulnerability Management and Risk Assessment

AI can assist organizations in identifying vulnerabilities in their cloud environments by continuously scanning configurations and applications for known security weaknesses. Machine learning models can prioritize vulnerabilities based on their potential impact and likelihood of exploitation, helping organizations focus their remediation efforts.

Action Item: Implement AI-driven vulnerability management tools that provide real-time assessments of cloud security postures.

Enhanced Data Protection and Encryption

AI can improve data protection measures by automating the process of data classification, identifying sensitive data that requires encryption, and applying the appropriate security controls. AI-driven encryption solutions can adapt to the data types and their usage patterns, ensuring that sensitive data remains protected even in dynamic cloud environments.

Example: An AI system can automatically identify personally identifiable information (PII) in cloud databases and enforce encryption policies to safeguard that data.

Best Practices for Implementing AI in Cloud Security

Integrate AI into Existing Security Frameworks

Organizations should integrate AI technologies into their existing security frameworks rather than treating them as standalone solutions. This approach ensures that AI complements existing security measures, enhancing overall security posture.

Action Item: Conduct an assessment of current security measures and identify areas where AI can provide additional value.

Choose the Right AI Tools and Solutions

Selecting the right AI tools and solutions is crucial for effective cloud security. Organizations should evaluate solutions based on their specific needs, considering factors such as scalability, ease of integration, and compatibility with existing systems.

Recommendation: Research vendors that offer AI-driven security solutions tailored for cloud environments and conduct thorough evaluations.

Ensure Transparency and Explainability

As organizations adopt AI for security purposes, it's essential to ensure transparency and explainability in AI decision-making processes. Security teams must understand how AI algorithms operate to build trust in their recommendations and actions.

Action Item: Seek AI solutions that provide insights into their decision-making processes, allowing security teams to understand the rationale behind alerts and recommendations.

Regularly Update and Train AI Models

Continuous improvement of AI models is necessary to keep pace with evolving threats. Organizations should regularly update and retrain their AI systems with new data to ensure their effectiveness.

Recommendation: Establish processes for periodically reviewing and updating AI models to enhance their accuracy and relevance.

Maintain a Focus on Compliance and Data Privacy

When implementing AI-driven security measures in the cloud, organizations must prioritize compliance with relevant data privacy regulations. This involves ensuring that AI systems handle sensitive data appropriately and adhere to legal requirements.

Action Item: Conduct regular audits to assess compliance with data protection regulations and adjust AI-driven security practices as needed.

Securing cloud infrastructures is a complex challenge that requires innovative solutions. AI offers powerful tools to enhance cloud security, providing organizations with the ability to detect threats, automate responses, and protect sensitive data more effectively. By understanding the challenges of cloud security and implementing AI-driven strategies, organizations can build a resilient security posture that safeguards their assets in an increasingly complex threat landscape.

As organizations continue to embrace cloud computing, leveraging AI in cloud security will be essential for mitigating risks and responding to the evolving threat landscape. By adopting best practices and integrating AI into their security frameworks, organizations can enhance their ability to defend against a wide range of cyber threats and ensure the security of their cloud environments.

10.2 AI's Role in Safeguarding Internet of Things (IoT) Devices

The Internet of Things (IoT) has revolutionized the way we interact with technology, enabling a wide array of devices to communicate and operate autonomously. From smart home appliances to industrial machinery, IoT devices offer unprecedented convenience and efficiency. However, this interconnectivity comes with significant security risks, as many IoT devices are vulnerable to cyberattacks. As the number of IoT devices continues to grow, the need for effective security measures has become paramount. Artificial intelligence (AI) is emerging as a critical tool in safeguarding IoT environments, offering advanced capabilities to identify, prevent, and respond to cyber threats.

Understanding the Security Challenges of IoT Devices

Limited Resources and Capabilities

Many IoT devices operate with limited computational power, memory, and battery life. This constraint often results in inadequate security measures, making them attractive targets for cybercriminals.

Example: A low-cost smart thermostat may lack the processing capability to implement advanced encryption or intrusion detection systems, leaving it susceptible to attacks.

Diverse Ecosystem of Devices

The IoT ecosystem consists of a vast array of devices from different manufacturers, each with unique operating systems, protocols, and security features. This diversity complicates security management and creates inconsistencies in security practices.

Challenge: A vulnerability in one device can expose the entire network, as many IoT devices are interconnected and can communicate with one another.

Inadequate Security Protocols

Many IoT devices are deployed with default security settings that are rarely changed by users. These default configurations often include weak passwords and unencrypted communication channels, making them easy targets for attackers.

Concern: Cybercriminals can exploit these weaknesses to gain unauthorized access to networks and sensitive data.

Data Privacy Concerns

IoT devices frequently collect and transmit sensitive personal data, raising privacy concerns. Ensuring that this data is securely transmitted and stored is critical to maintaining user trust.

Implication: A data breach involving IoT devices can lead to significant privacy violations and regulatory penalties.

The Role of AI in Securing IoT Devices

Anomaly Detection and Threat Identification

AI can analyze the behavior of IoT devices in real-time to detect anomalies that may indicate potential security threats. By establishing baselines for normal device behavior, AI systems can identify unusual patterns that may suggest an attack or compromise.

Example: An AI-driven security system can monitor the communication patterns of smart home devices and alert users if a device begins transmitting data to an unfamiliar IP address.

Predictive Threat Modeling

Machine learning algorithms can be used to create predictive models that assess the likelihood of potential threats to IoT devices. By analyzing historical attack data and identifying common attack vectors, AI can help organizations prioritize their security efforts.

Benefit: Organizations can focus their resources on protecting the most vulnerable devices and systems, reducing the risk of successful attacks.

Automated Response and Mitigation

AI can facilitate automated responses to security incidents involving IoT devices. For instance, if an anomaly is detected, an AI system can automatically isolate the compromised device from the network, preventing further damage.

Action Item: Implement AI-driven security solutions that can autonomously respond to detected threats, reducing the need for manual intervention and speeding up response times.

Enhanced Authentication Mechanisms

AI can improve authentication processes for IoT devices by implementing adaptive authentication mechanisms that evaluate user behavior and context. This approach allows for dynamic authentication that adjusts based on risk levels.

Example: An AI system could require additional authentication factors if a user attempts to access an IoT device from an unusual location or device.

Vulnerability Management and Patch Automation

AI can assist in identifying vulnerabilities in IoT devices by continuously scanning for known security flaws and recommending patches or updates. This capability is crucial for maintaining the security of devices that may not have built-in patch management features.

Action Item: Deploy AI-driven vulnerability management tools that can automatically detect and remediate security vulnerabilities in IoT devices.

Data Encryption and Secure Communication

AI can enhance the security of data transmitted by IoT devices through automated encryption processes. By ensuring that data is encrypted before transmission, organizations can protect sensitive information from being intercepted by attackers.

Example: An AI system could automatically enforce encryption standards for data transmitted between IoT devices and cloud services.

Behavioral Biometrics for User Authentication

Behavioral biometrics is an emerging area where AI analyzes patterns in user behavior—such as typing speed, mouse movements, and interaction patterns—to authenticate users. This method can add an additional layer of security for IoT devices.

Benefit: By utilizing behavioral biometrics, organizations can enhance user authentication processes, making it more difficult for unauthorized users to gain access.

Security Information and Event Management (SIEM)

AI can enhance Security Information and Event Management (SIEM) systems by providing real-time analysis of security alerts generated by various IoT devices. By correlating data from multiple sources, AI can identify patterns that might indicate a coordinated attack.

Action Item: Integrate AI capabilities into existing SIEM solutions to improve threat detection and incident response capabilities.

Continuous Learning and Adaptation

One of the significant advantages of AI is its ability to continuously learn from new data and adapt to evolving threats. As cybercriminals develop new tactics, AI systems can refine their models and improve their defenses accordingly.

Example: An AI-driven security solution can learn from recent attacks against IoT devices and update its detection algorithms to identify similar threats in the future.

Collaboration and Threat Intelligence Sharing

AI can facilitate collaboration and information sharing among organizations regarding IoT security threats. By leveraging collective threat intelligence, organizations can enhance their security measures and stay informed about emerging risks.

Action Item: Participate in threat intelligence sharing initiatives to benefit from insights into vulnerabilities and threats affecting IoT devices.

Best Practices for Implementing AI in IoT Security

Adopt a Layered Security Approach

Implement a multi-layered security strategy that combines AI-driven solutions with traditional security measures. This approach ensures comprehensive protection against a wide range of threats.

Recommendation: Utilize a combination of AI-driven anomaly detection, encryption, and access controls to create a robust security framework for IoT devices.

Conduct Regular Security Audits

Regular security audits of IoT devices and networks are essential for identifying vulnerabilities and ensuring compliance with security standards. AI can assist in automating parts of this process, making it more efficient.

Action Item: Schedule routine audits to assess the security posture of IoT devices and identify areas for improvement.

Ensure Compliance with Security Standards

Organizations must ensure that their IoT devices comply with industry standards and regulations regarding security and data privacy. This compliance helps build trust with users and reduces legal risks.

Action Item: Review relevant security standards and regulations to ensure that IoT security measures align with compliance requirements.

Invest in Employee Training and Awareness

Employees play a crucial role in maintaining IoT security. Providing training on best practices for using and securing IoT devices can significantly reduce the risk of human error leading to security breaches.

Action Item: Develop training programs that educate employees about the importance of IoT security and the specific risks associated with IoT devices.

Foster a Security-First Culture

Building a security-first culture within the organization encourages all employees to prioritize security in their daily operations. This mindset can help identify potential threats and promote proactive security measures.

Action Item: Encourage open communication about security concerns and promote best practices across all levels of the organization.

AI is playing an increasingly vital role in safeguarding IoT devices from cyber threats. By leveraging AI's capabilities in anomaly detection, predictive modeling, automated responses, and continuous learning, organizations can enhance their ability to protect their IoT environments. As the IoT landscape continues to expand, adopting AI-driven security measures will be essential for mitigating risks and ensuring the secure operation of interconnected devices.

By understanding the challenges associated with IoT security and implementing best practices for AI integration, organizations can build a resilient security posture that safeguards their IoT devices and protects sensitive data. As cyber threats evolve, the importance of AI in securing IoT infrastructures will only grow, making it a critical component of any comprehensive cybersecurity strategy.

10.3 Vulnerabilities and Threats in Smart Networks and Connected Ecosystems

The proliferation of smart networks and connected ecosystems has transformed various sectors, including smart cities, healthcare, transportation, and manufacturing. These interconnected systems offer remarkable efficiency and convenience, allowing devices and systems to communicate and operate collaboratively. However, this interconnectivity also introduces significant vulnerabilities and threats, making smart networks attractive targets for cybercriminals. This chapter delves into the vulnerabilities associated with smart networks, the types of threats they face, and strategies for mitigating these risks.

Understanding Smart Networks and Connected Ecosystems

Definition and Components

Smart networks comprise interconnected devices that collect, exchange, and analyze data to optimize operations and improve decision-making. These ecosystems often integrate Internet of Things (IoT) devices, cloud computing, artificial intelligence (AI), and data analytics to create responsive environments.

Examples: Smart cities utilize connected sensors for traffic management, while smart homes employ devices like smart thermostats, security cameras, and smart appliances.

Interconnectivity and Complexity

The interconnected nature of smart networks increases their complexity, making it challenging to implement uniform security measures. The reliance on multiple vendors and technologies can lead to inconsistent security practices across devices and platforms.

Challenge: A single vulnerability in one component of the network can compromise the entire ecosystem.

Vulnerabilities in Smart Networks

Insecure Device Interfaces

Many IoT devices have poorly designed interfaces that lack robust security measures. These interfaces may be vulnerable to exploitation, allowing unauthorized access and control over connected devices.

Example: A smart lock may have a weak authentication mechanism, enabling attackers to gain access to a property by exploiting the device's interface.

Weak Authentication and Access Control

Weak passwords, default credentials, and inadequate access controls are common vulnerabilities in smart devices. Attackers can easily exploit these weaknesses to gain unauthorized access to networks and data.

Concern: Many users fail to change default passwords, making devices easy targets for automated attacks.

Data Transmission Vulnerabilities

Data transmitted between devices in smart networks may not be adequately encrypted, making it susceptible to interception and tampering. Attackers can exploit these vulnerabilities to eavesdrop on communications or manipulate data.

Example: An unencrypted transmission between a smart thermostat and a cloud server can be intercepted, allowing attackers to gain insights into users' behaviors.

Firmware and Software Vulnerabilities

Many IoT devices rely on outdated firmware and software that may contain unpatched vulnerabilities. Manufacturers often provide limited support for their devices, leading to security gaps that cybercriminals can exploit.

Action Item: Regularly updating firmware and software is essential for maintaining security, but many users neglect this task.

Inadequate Network Security

Smart networks often lack robust network segmentation and security controls, exposing devices to potential threats. Without proper network security measures, attackers can move laterally within the network to exploit other vulnerable devices.

Example: An attacker who compromises a smart light bulb may gain access to the entire home network if no segmentation is in place.

Types of Threats to Smart Networks

Malware Attacks

Malware designed specifically for IoT devices can disrupt operations, steal data, or turn devices into part of a botnet. These attacks can have widespread consequences, affecting not only the targeted devices but also the broader network.

Example: The Mirai botnet used compromised IoT devices to launch large-scale Distributed Denial of Service (DDoS) attacks, demonstrating the potential for widespread disruption.

Denial of Service (DoS) Attacks

DoS attacks aim to overwhelm smart networks by flooding them with traffic, rendering devices and services unavailable. Such attacks can disrupt critical infrastructure, leading to significant operational impacts.

Concern: Smart cities relying on connected services for traffic management can experience severe disruptions during a DoS attack.

Data Breaches

Cybercriminals may target smart networks to access sensitive data, such as personal information, financial records, or proprietary business data. Data breaches can have severe implications for individuals and organizations, including reputational damage and financial losses.

Example: A breach of a healthcare IoT system may expose patients' medical records, violating privacy regulations and eroding trust.

Man-in-the-Middle (MitM) Attacks

In MitM attacks, cybercriminals intercept communications between devices to eavesdrop, modify data, or impersonate devices. These attacks can compromise the integrity and confidentiality of data transmitted within smart networks.

Example: An attacker may intercept data transmitted between a smart home security system and its mobile app, gaining access to sensitive information.

Physical Attacks

Physical access to IoT devices can enable attackers to manipulate or compromise them. Smart devices are often deployed in public or unsecured locations, making them vulnerable to tampering.

Action Item: Implementing physical security measures, such as tamper-resistant enclosures, can help protect devices from physical threats.

Mitigating Vulnerabilities and Threats in Smart Networks

Implement Strong Authentication and Access Controls

Organizations should enforce strong authentication mechanisms, such as two-factor authentication (2FA), and implement strict access controls to limit who can access devices and data.

Action Item: Regularly review user access permissions and ensure that they align with the principle of least privilege.

Enhance Device Security Protocols

Manufacturers should prioritize security when designing devices by implementing secure coding practices and robust security protocols. This includes ensuring that devices support encryption and secure communication methods.

Recommendation: Encourage manufacturers to adopt industry standards for device security.

Regular Software and Firmware Updates

Organizations and users must prioritize regular updates to firmware and software to address known vulnerabilities. Automated update mechanisms can help ensure that devices remain secure without requiring manual intervention.

Action Item: Develop a policy for regularly checking and applying updates to all devices in the network.

Network Segmentation and Monitoring

Segmenting networks can help contain potential breaches and limit lateral movement within the ecosystem. Implementing network monitoring solutions can also help identify unusual behavior and potential threats.

Example: Use virtual LANs (VLANs) to separate IoT devices from critical systems and data.

Conduct Regular Security Assessments

Regular security assessments, including penetration testing and vulnerability scanning, can help organizations identify weaknesses in their smart networks and take corrective actions.

Action Item: Schedule routine security assessments to evaluate the effectiveness of security measures and identify areas for improvement.

Educate Users and Stakeholders

Educating users about the risks associated with smart networks and best practices for securing devices is crucial for reducing vulnerabilities. Organizations should provide training and resources to help users understand their role in maintaining security.

Action Item: Develop training programs that educate users on recognizing phishing attempts, changing default passwords, and securing devices.

Foster Collaboration and Information Sharing

Collaboration among organizations, manufacturers, and cybersecurity experts can enhance the overall security posture of smart networks. Sharing information about threats and vulnerabilities can help organizations stay informed and better prepared.

Recommendation: Participate in industry initiatives and forums focused on sharing threat intelligence and best practices for IoT security.

The vulnerabilities and threats associated with smart networks and connected ecosystems present significant challenges for organizations and individuals alike. As the reliance on interconnected devices continues to grow, so does the need for effective security measures. By understanding the vulnerabilities inherent in smart networks and implementing strategies to mitigate threats, organizations can enhance their resilience against cyberattacks.

AI plays a crucial role in addressing these challenges, providing advanced capabilities for threat detection, response, and vulnerability management. By adopting a proactive security approach and fostering a culture of awareness and collaboration, organizations can safeguard their smart networks and connected ecosystems from emerging threats, ensuring the continued benefits of these innovative technologies.

Chapter 11: The Future of AI and Cybersecurity: Trends and Predictions

In this chapter, we look ahead to the future of artificial intelligence in cybersecurity, exploring emerging trends and making informed predictions about the evolving landscape. As technology continues to advance at an unprecedented pace, we analyze how developments such as quantum computing may impact AI-driven security measures, potentially rendering traditional encryption methods obsolete. We discuss the rise of autonomous security systems that leverage AI to not only detect and respond to threats but also to learn and adapt in real-time, creating a more proactive defense framework. Additionally, we examine the growing importance of collaboration between AI systems and human cybersecurity experts, emphasizing the need for a balanced approach that harnesses the strengths of both. This chapter also considers the ethical and regulatory implications of AI in cybersecurity, including the need for frameworks that ensure responsible AI usage. By identifying these trends and potential challenges, we aim to provide a roadmap for organizations looking to navigate the future of cybersecurity, equipping them with the insights necessary to remain resilient against the threats that lie ahead.

11.1 Quantum Computing's Impact on AI-Driven Security

Quantum computing represents a significant leap forward in computational power, leveraging the principles of quantum mechanics to process information in ways that classical computers cannot. This emerging technology has profound implications for various fields, including artificial intelligence (AI) and cybersecurity. As organizations increasingly rely on AI-driven security solutions to protect their digital assets, the advent of quantum computing poses both opportunities and challenges. This chapter explores how quantum computing impacts AI-driven security, examining the potential benefits and risks associated with this transformative technology.

Understanding Quantum Computing

Fundamental Principles of Quantum Computing

Quantum computing is based on the principles of quantum mechanics, particularly the concepts of superposition and entanglement. Unlike classical bits, which can exist in one of two states (0 or 1), quantum bits, or qubits, can exist in multiple states simultaneously, allowing quantum computers to perform complex calculations at unprecedented speeds.

Superposition: A qubit can represent both 0 and 1 at the same time, enabling parallel processing of information.

Entanglement: Qubits can be interconnected, such that the state of one qubit can depend on the state of another, allowing for faster information transfer and processing.

Potential Capabilities of Quantum Computers

Quantum computers are expected to excel in solving specific problems that are currently intractable for classical computers. This includes tasks such as factoring large integers, optimizing complex systems, and simulating quantum processes.

Example: Shor's algorithm, a quantum algorithm, can factor large numbers exponentially faster than the best-known classical algorithms, posing a potential threat to traditional cryptographic systems.

The Intersection of Quantum Computing and AI

Enhancing AI Algorithms with Quantum Computing

Quantum computing has the potential to enhance AI algorithms by providing faster processing capabilities and improved optimization techniques. Quantum machine learning (QML) combines quantum computing with traditional machine learning methods to create more efficient models and algorithms.

Example: Quantum algorithms can process vast datasets more efficiently, enabling faster training of machine learning models and improved predictive capabilities.

Accelerating Data Processing and Analysis

The ability of quantum computers to perform complex calculations quickly can significantly accelerate data processing and analysis in AI-driven security systems. This speed can enhance threat detection, anomaly identification, and predictive analytics.

Benefit: Organizations can respond to emerging threats more rapidly, improving their overall security posture.

Improving Encryption Techniques

Quantum computing could lead to the development of new encryption techniques that are more secure against quantum attacks. Quantum key distribution (QKD) uses the principles of quantum mechanics to create secure communication channels that are theoretically invulnerable to eavesdropping.

Example: QKD allows parties to share encryption keys securely, ensuring that even if an attacker intercepts the transmission, they cannot decipher the key without disturbing the quantum state.

Challenges Posed by Quantum Computing to AI-Driven Security

Threats to Traditional Cryptography

One of the most significant challenges posed by quantum computing is its potential to break existing cryptographic systems. Classical encryption methods, such as RSA and ECC, rely on the difficulty of factoring large numbers or solving discrete logarithm problems, tasks that quantum computers can perform efficiently.

Implication: Organizations that rely on classical encryption methods may need to transition to quantum-resistant algorithms to safeguard sensitive data.

Evolving AI Threat Landscape

As quantum computing becomes more accessible, malicious actors may harness its power to develop advanced cyberattack techniques. Quantum-enhanced attacks could enable adversaries to bypass traditional security measures, making it critical for organizations to stay ahead of these emerging threats.

Example: Quantum computers could be used to generate sophisticated phishing attacks or break password hashes faster than traditional computing methods.

Increased Complexity in Security Management

The integration of quantum computing into AI-driven security systems introduces additional complexity in security management. Organizations will need to adapt their security strategies to account for the unique challenges posed by quantum computing while ensuring their existing systems remain secure.

Challenge: Organizations may need to invest in specialized knowledge and training to effectively manage quantum-enhanced security risks.

Strategies for Preparing for Quantum Computing's Impact

Adopting Quantum-Resistant Algorithms

Organizations should begin transitioning to quantum-resistant cryptographic algorithms to safeguard sensitive data and communications. This proactive approach will help mitigate the risks associated with potential quantum attacks.

Action Item: Monitor developments in quantum-resistant cryptography and collaborate with standards organizations to implement best practices.

Investing in Quantum Security Solutions

Organizations should explore quantum security solutions, such as quantum key distribution, to enhance their encryption capabilities. By leveraging quantum technologies, organizations can create more secure communication channels.

Recommendation: Evaluate quantum security offerings and consider pilot projects to assess their effectiveness in enhancing data security.

Continuous Monitoring and Threat Intelligence

Organizations must implement robust monitoring and threat intelligence capabilities to detect emerging threats related to quantum computing. Staying informed about advancements in quantum technologies and their implications for cybersecurity is essential.

Action Item: Participate in threat intelligence sharing initiatives focused on quantum-related vulnerabilities and risks.

Enhancing Collaboration Across Industries

Collaboration among industry stakeholders, researchers, and cybersecurity experts is crucial for addressing the challenges posed by quantum computing. Sharing insights and best practices can help organizations collectively prepare for the impact of quantum technologies.

Recommendation: Engage in cross-industry forums and initiatives aimed at exploring the intersection of quantum computing and cybersecurity.

Investing in Research and Development

Organizations should invest in research and development efforts focused on quantum computing and its implications for AI-driven security. Understanding the potential impact of quantum technologies will enable organizations to adapt their strategies effectively.

Action Item: Collaborate with academic institutions and research organizations to explore the latest advancements in quantum computing and cybersecurity.

Quantum computing represents a transformative force in the field of cybersecurity, with the potential to enhance AI-driven security solutions while simultaneously posing significant risks. Organizations must proactively prepare for the impact of quantum technologies by adopting quantum-resistant algorithms, exploring quantum security solutions, and enhancing their monitoring capabilities.

As quantum computing continues to evolve, its intersection with AI will reshape the cybersecurity landscape. By understanding the challenges and opportunities presented by quantum computing, organizations can position themselves to navigate the complexities of this new era in cybersecurity effectively. The collaboration between AI and quantum computing will play a crucial role in building resilient security systems capable of defending against the threats of tomorrow.

11.2 Autonomous Security Systems: Can AI Defend Itself?

The rise of autonomous security systems powered by artificial intelligence (AI) has transformed how organizations approach cybersecurity. These systems, capable of independently detecting, responding to, and mitigating threats, promise to enhance security protocols and provide real-time defense against cyberattacks. However, as the capabilities of AI-driven systems evolve, an intriguing question arises: can AI defend itself? This chapter delves into the mechanisms and implications of autonomous security systems, exploring their strengths, limitations, and the critical considerations surrounding AI's ability to protect itself against evolving threats.

Understanding Autonomous Security Systems

Definition and Features of Autonomous Security Systems

Autonomous security systems refer to AI-driven solutions designed to operate independently, analyzing data, identifying threats, and executing responses without direct human intervention. These systems leverage machine learning, deep learning, and natural language processing to continuously improve their capabilities.

Key Features:

- **Self-learning**: The ability to learn from past experiences and adapt to new threats.
- **Real-time response**: Immediate action in response to detected threats, reducing reaction time.
- **Automated processes**: Minimizing human involvement in routine security tasks.

Components of Autonomous Security Systems

Autonomous security systems typically consist of several interconnected components that work together to ensure comprehensive protection:

- **Data collection and analysis**: Gathering data from various sources, such as network traffic, user behavior, and system logs, to identify potential threats.
- **Threat detection**: Utilizing machine learning algorithms to analyze data patterns and detect anomalies indicative of security breaches.
- **Incident response**: Automatically executing predefined protocols to mitigate detected threats, such as isolating affected systems or blocking malicious traffic.

The Self-Defense Capability of AI

Self-Learning and Adaptation

One of the most significant advantages of AI-driven security systems is their ability to learn from previous attacks and adapt their defenses accordingly. This self-learning capability enables autonomous systems to improve their threat detection and response mechanisms over time.

Example: If a new type of phishing attack is detected, the AI system can analyze the characteristics of the attack and update its algorithms to recognize similar threats in the future.

Automated Threat Hunting

Autonomous security systems can continuously monitor network environments for potential threats, proactively hunting for indicators of compromise (IoCs). This automated threat-hunting capability allows AI to stay ahead of attackers by identifying vulnerabilities before they can be exploited.

Benefit: By maintaining a constant watch over network activity, AI can effectively defend against zero-day attacks and other emerging threats.

Incident Response Automation

In the event of a detected threat, autonomous security systems can initiate automated incident response protocols. This rapid response reduces the time it takes to contain and mitigate threats, minimizing potential damage.

Example: An AI system detecting a DDoS attack can automatically reroute traffic to mitigate the attack's impact without human intervention.

Self-Assessment and Vulnerability Management

Advanced AI security systems can conduct self-assessments to identify potential vulnerabilities in their own configurations and algorithms. By recognizing and addressing weaknesses, these systems can enhance their resilience against attacks.

Action Item: Regular self-assessment protocols allow AI systems to maintain robust defenses and adapt to evolving threat landscapes.

Limitations of Autonomous Security Systems

Dependence on Training Data

The effectiveness of AI-driven security systems hinges on the quality and comprehensiveness of the training data they receive. If the training data is biased or incomplete, the system's ability to recognize threats can be compromised.

Concern: An AI system trained on a narrow dataset may fail to detect novel or sophisticated attacks that deviate from known patterns.

Vulnerabilities to Adversarial Attacks

Autonomous security systems are not immune to adversarial attacks, where malicious actors manipulate input data to deceive the AI. These attacks can lead to incorrect classifications and missed threats, undermining the system's effectiveness.

Example: An attacker could introduce subtle modifications to network traffic that lead the AI system to misidentify malicious activity as benign.

Limitations in Contextual Understanding

While AI excels at pattern recognition, it often lacks the contextual understanding that human analysts bring to cybersecurity. This limitation can hinder the system's ability to make nuanced decisions in complex situations.

Challenge: An AI system may misinterpret benign activities as threats due to its inability to understand the broader context of the situation.

Ethical and Accountability Concerns

As AI systems take on more autonomous roles in security, ethical considerations regarding accountability and decision-making arise. Questions about who is responsible for the actions taken by autonomous systems in the event of a failure or breach need careful consideration.

Implication: Organizations must establish clear guidelines and frameworks for accountability in the deployment of autonomous security systems.

Enhancing AI's Defensive Capabilities

Continuous Learning and Improvement

Organizations should implement mechanisms for continuous learning, enabling autonomous security systems to evolve with the threat landscape. Regular updates to training data and algorithms can enhance the system's adaptability.

Action Item: Establish a feedback loop where the AI system learns from new threats and integrates insights gained from human analysts.

Collaboration with Human Analysts

While autonomous systems can handle routine tasks, collaboration with human analysts is essential for addressing complex threats. Combining human intuition and expertise with AI's processing power can create a more robust security posture.

Benefit: Human oversight ensures that AI systems operate effectively and adapt to nuanced situations that may require contextual understanding.

Implementing Robust Testing and Validation

Rigorous testing and validation protocols are critical to ensure the reliability of autonomous security systems. Organizations should conduct regular assessments to identify vulnerabilities and improve system performance.

Action Item: Develop a comprehensive testing strategy that includes simulated attacks and real-world scenarios to evaluate the effectiveness of the AI system.

Ethical Frameworks for AI Decision-Making

Establishing ethical frameworks for AI decision-making can help organizations navigate the complexities of autonomous security systems. Clear guidelines for accountability and transparency can foster trust and ensure responsible use of AI.

Recommendation: Collaborate with stakeholders to develop ethical standards that govern the deployment and operation of autonomous security systems.

Autonomous security systems powered by AI represent a transformative shift in cybersecurity, enabling organizations to enhance their defenses against an increasingly complex threat landscape. While these systems possess remarkable capabilities for self-learning, automated threat detection, and incident response, they also face limitations that must be addressed.

The question of whether AI can defend itself hinges on its ability to adapt, learn, and collaborate effectively with human analysts. By fostering continuous improvement, enhancing collaboration, and establishing ethical frameworks, organizations can unlock the full potential of autonomous security systems. As AI-driven security evolves, it will play a pivotal role in shaping the future of cybersecurity, enabling organizations to stay ahead of emerging threats and fortify their defenses in an ever-changing digital landscape.

11.3 Self-Healing Networks: The Next Step in AI-Driven Cyber Defense

The concept of self-healing networks represents a groundbreaking advancement in the realm of cybersecurity, where systems autonomously detect, respond to, and recover from anomalies and threats without human intervention. This innovative approach integrates artificial intelligence (AI) with network management, enabling organizations to create resilient infrastructures capable of self-repair. As cyber threats continue to evolve in complexity and scale, self-healing networks promise to be a critical component of AI-driven cyber defense strategies. This chapter explores the fundamental principles, benefits, challenges, and future prospects of self-healing networks in enhancing cybersecurity.

Understanding Self-Healing Networks

Definition and Core Principles

Self-healing networks are designed to autonomously detect, diagnose, and remediate issues within their infrastructure. By leveraging AI and machine learning algorithms, these networks continuously monitor their operations, allowing them to identify irregularities that could signify potential threats or failures.

Key Characteristics:

- **Autonomous detection**: The ability to recognize issues without human oversight.
- **Root cause analysis**: Analyzing the underlying causes of detected problems to implement effective solutions.
- **Automated remediation**: Instantly taking corrective actions to resolve identified issues and restore normal operations.

Components of Self-Healing Networks

A self-healing network typically consists of several interrelated components that work together to ensure seamless operation:

- **Monitoring and Analytics**: Continuous observation of network activity and performance metrics to identify anomalies.
- **Artificial Intelligence Algorithms**: Machine learning models that analyze data patterns to detect deviations and predict potential issues.

- **Automated Response Mechanisms**: Predefined protocols that the network employs to rectify problems, such as rerouting traffic, restarting services, or applying security patches.

Benefits of Self-Healing Networks

Enhanced Resilience and Reliability

Self-healing networks can significantly improve the resilience of IT infrastructures by minimizing downtime and ensuring continuous availability of services. The automated remediation processes allow organizations to quickly recover from disruptions caused by cyberattacks, hardware failures, or configuration errors.

Example: In the event of a denial-of-service (DoS) attack, a self-healing network can automatically redirect traffic to alternative pathways, thereby maintaining service availability for legitimate users.

Reduction of Human Error

By automating network management tasks, self-healing networks reduce the reliance on human intervention, thereby decreasing the likelihood of errors that can exacerbate security vulnerabilities. Automation also allows IT staff to focus on strategic initiatives rather than routine troubleshooting.

Benefit: This not only enhances security but also optimizes resource allocation within the IT team.

Faster Incident Response

The ability to autonomously identify and address threats enables self-healing networks to respond to incidents much more rapidly than traditional systems. This quick response is crucial in mitigating the impact of cyberattacks and preventing data breaches.

Example: If a network anomaly indicative of a breach is detected, the self-healing system can immediately isolate affected segments and initiate containment protocols.

Continuous Learning and Improvement

Self-healing networks incorporate machine learning capabilities that allow them to continuously learn from past incidents and improve their detection and response strategies. By analyzing historical data, these networks can identify patterns that lead to vulnerabilities and implement measures to address them proactively.

Action Item: This feedback loop fosters a culture of continuous improvement, ensuring that the network evolves alongside emerging threats.

Challenges of Implementing Self-Healing Networks

Complexity of Integration

Integrating self-healing capabilities into existing network infrastructures can be complex and resource-intensive. Organizations may face challenges in aligning legacy systems with modern self-healing technologies, requiring significant investment in time and resources.

Concern: Legacy systems may not support the advanced monitoring and analytics required for effective self-healing operations.

Over-Reliance on Automation

While automation enhances efficiency, over-reliance on self-healing mechanisms can lead to complacency among IT staff. Organizations must maintain a balance between automated responses and human oversight to ensure that critical decisions are not left solely to machines.

Challenge: Ensuring that human analysts remain engaged and prepared to intervene in complex situations is essential for comprehensive security management.

Potential for False Positives

Self-healing networks may encounter issues with false positives, where benign activities are misidentified as threats. This can lead to unnecessary interruptions and disruptions in service, ultimately affecting user experience and trust.

Implication: Organizations must fine-tune their algorithms to minimize false positives while maintaining robust detection capabilities.

Security Concerns of AI Algorithms

The AI algorithms that underpin self-healing networks can also be targeted by adversaries. Malicious actors may attempt to manipulate these algorithms, leading to unintended consequences and potentially compromising network security.

Example: An attacker could exploit vulnerabilities in the AI model to create conditions that trigger self-healing responses in ways that facilitate further breaches.

Future Prospects of Self-Healing Networks

Advancements in AI and Machine Learning

As AI and machine learning technologies continue to evolve, self-healing networks are expected to become more sophisticated and capable of addressing increasingly complex threats. Enhanced algorithms will improve detection accuracy and response efficacy, making these networks integral to future cybersecurity strategies.

Benefit: Organizations can leverage the latest advancements in AI to bolster their defenses against emerging threats.

Integration with Zero Trust Architectures

Self-healing networks can be integrated into zero trust security models, where no user or device is inherently trusted, and access is continually evaluated. This integration allows for dynamic adjustments to access controls based on real-time threat assessments.

Example: If a user's behavior deviates from established patterns, the self-healing network can automatically adjust their access privileges until the situation is resolved.

Collaboration with Other Security Technologies

Self-healing networks can work in conjunction with other cybersecurity technologies, such as threat intelligence platforms and behavioral analytics tools, to create a comprehensive security ecosystem. This collaboration enhances the overall effectiveness of an organization's security posture.

Action Item: Organizations should explore opportunities to integrate self-healing capabilities with existing security solutions for a more holistic approach to cybersecurity.

Continuous Evolution of Security Protocols

The threat landscape is dynamic and constantly evolving. As cyberattacks grow in sophistication, self-healing networks will need to adapt their protocols to ensure ongoing effectiveness. This evolution will require regular updates to AI models and security strategies.

Recommendation: Organizations should establish a proactive framework for regularly updating their self-healing systems to align with the latest threat intelligence and security practices.

Self-healing networks represent a significant advancement in AI-driven cyber defense, offering organizations the ability to autonomously detect, respond to, and recover from cyber threats. With their enhanced resilience, reduced reliance on human intervention, and continuous learning capabilities, self-healing networks are poised to play a crucial role in the future of cybersecurity.

However, the implementation of these networks comes with challenges that organizations must navigate, including complexity, potential over-reliance on automation, and the need to fine-tune detection algorithms. By proactively addressing these challenges and investing in continuous improvement, organizations can harness the full potential of self-healing networks to create a more robust and adaptive cybersecurity posture. As the landscape of cyber threats continues to evolve, the integration of self-healing networks will be vital for organizations seeking to stay ahead of adversaries and ensure the integrity of their digital infrastructures.

Chapter 12: Building a Symbiotic Defense System

In this final chapter, we synthesize the insights gained throughout the book to explore the concept of a symbiotic defense system, where artificial intelligence and human expertise work in harmony to enhance cybersecurity. We begin by discussing the importance of integrating AI technologies into existing security frameworks, emphasizing that AI should augment—not replace—human decision-making. This chapter outlines best practices for organizations seeking to develop a balanced approach, including strategies for fostering collaboration between AI systems and security teams. We delve into the design of adaptive and self-learning security architectures that can evolve in response to new threats, highlighting the role of continuous learning and improvement. Furthermore, we examine case studies of organizations that have successfully implemented symbiotic defense systems, showcasing the tangible benefits of this approach in real-world scenarios. Finally, we look ahead to the future, encouraging organizations to embrace innovation and adaptability as they navigate the complexities of cybersecurity in an increasingly digital world. By building a symbiotic defense system, organizations can create a resilient security posture that leverages the strengths of both AI and human intelligence to effectively combat the ever-evolving landscape of cyber threats.

12.1 Integrating AI with Human Expertise for a Balanced Defense

In the rapidly evolving landscape of cybersecurity, the integration of artificial intelligence (AI) with human expertise has emerged as a cornerstone of effective defense strategies. While AI systems excel at processing vast amounts of data, identifying patterns, and automating responses, they lack the contextual understanding, intuition, and ethical reasoning that human professionals bring to the table. This chapter explores the importance of a balanced approach that combines the strengths of AI with the irreplaceable insights of human analysts, ultimately fostering a more robust and adaptive cybersecurity framework.

Understanding the Roles of AI and Human Expertise

The Strengths of AI in Cybersecurity

AI technologies have transformed the cybersecurity landscape by enabling organizations to analyze data at an unprecedented scale and speed. Some of the key strengths of AI include:

- **Data Processing and Analysis**: AI systems can sift through vast amounts of network data, logs, and threat intelligence in real-time to identify potential threats and anomalies that may go unnoticed by human analysts.
- **Pattern Recognition**: Through machine learning algorithms, AI can recognize complex patterns and correlations in data that indicate potential security breaches or vulnerabilities.
- **Automation of Routine Tasks**: AI can automate repetitive tasks, such as monitoring network traffic and responding to alerts, allowing human analysts to focus on more strategic and complex issues.

The Value of Human Expertise

Despite the advancements in AI, human analysts remain indispensable in the cybersecurity domain. Their unique strengths include:

- **Contextual Understanding**: Human professionals can interpret the context of security incidents, considering organizational nuances, industry-specific threats, and the intent behind certain actions that AI may not fully grasp.
- **Critical Thinking and Judgment**: Humans can apply critical thinking to assess threats, prioritize incidents, and make nuanced decisions that consider ethical implications and potential consequences.
- **Collaboration and Communication**: Human analysts excel at collaborating with different teams and communicating findings, insights, and strategies to various stakeholders, including technical and non-technical audiences.

Creating a Synergistic Relationship

Enhancing Human Decision-Making with AI

One of the most powerful aspects of integrating AI with human expertise is the ability to augment human decision-making. AI can provide valuable insights and recommendations based on data analysis, which can inform and guide human analysts in their assessments and actions.

Example: An AI system might flag a particular user behavior as suspicious, prompting a human analyst to investigate further. The analyst can then use their contextual understanding to determine whether the activity is genuinely malicious or a benign anomaly.

Using AI for Threat Intelligence and Research

AI can assist human analysts in gathering and synthesizing threat intelligence, providing them with timely information on emerging threats and attack trends. This capability allows human experts to stay informed and adapt their strategies accordingly.

Benefit: By automating the collection and analysis of threat data, AI frees up human analysts to focus on interpreting findings, developing proactive measures, and enhancing the organization's overall security posture.

Collaborative Incident Response

In incident response scenarios, the collaboration between AI and human experts can significantly enhance the effectiveness and speed of remediation efforts. While AI can automate initial detection and response steps, human analysts can provide context and make informed decisions about the best course of action.

Example: During a security breach, AI might isolate affected systems and block malicious IP addresses, while human analysts assess the broader impact, communicate with stakeholders, and implement long-term corrective actions.

Challenges and Considerations

Avoiding Over-Reliance on AI

One of the key challenges in integrating AI with human expertise is the risk of over-reliance on automated systems. While AI can enhance efficiency and effectiveness, it is crucial for organizations to maintain a strong human presence in cybersecurity operations to ensure comprehensive defense.

Concern: An over-reliance on AI could lead to complacency, where human analysts neglect their responsibilities in favor of deferring to automated systems, ultimately compromising security.

Training and Skill Development

To maximize the benefits of AI integration, organizations must invest in training and skill development for their cybersecurity personnel. This includes not only training on AI tools and technologies but also fostering critical thinking, problem-solving, and communication skills.

Action Item: Organizations should create training programs that emphasize the complementary roles of AI and human expertise, ensuring that analysts are equipped to leverage AI insights effectively.

Ethical Implications and Accountability

The integration of AI in cybersecurity raises important ethical considerations, particularly regarding accountability in decision-making. Organizations must establish clear frameworks for accountability, ensuring that human analysts remain responsible for the outcomes of AI-driven actions.

Recommendation: Create policies that delineate the responsibilities of AI systems and human analysts, including protocols for addressing errors or unintended consequences resulting from automated decisions.

Implementing a Balanced Defense Strategy

Developing an Integrated Security Framework

Organizations should develop an integrated security framework that emphasizes the collaboration between AI and human experts. This framework should outline roles, responsibilities, and processes for effective threat detection, response, and recovery.

Key Elements:

- **Defined roles**: Clearly delineate the roles of AI systems and human analysts in security operations.
- **Collaborative processes**: Establish protocols for how AI insights will inform human decision-making and vice versa.

Continuous Feedback and Improvement

A successful integration of AI and human expertise requires continuous feedback and improvement. Organizations should regularly assess the effectiveness of their integrated approach, identifying areas for enhancement and ensuring that both AI systems and human analysts are continually evolving.

Action Item: Implement feedback loops where human analysts can provide insights on AI performance, enabling organizations to refine algorithms and improve overall effectiveness.

Promoting a Culture of Collaboration

Fostering a culture of collaboration between AI and human analysts is essential for maximizing the benefits of their integration. Organizations should encourage open communication, knowledge sharing, and teamwork among their cybersecurity personnel.

Benefit: A collaborative environment enhances trust and encourages analysts to leverage AI insights effectively, leading to more informed decision-making and improved security outcomes.

The integration of AI with human expertise represents a critical evolution in the field of cybersecurity. By harnessing the strengths of both AI and human analysts, organizations can create a balanced defense strategy that enhances threat detection, response, and recovery capabilities.

However, this integration requires careful consideration of the challenges involved, including the risk of over-reliance on AI, the need for ongoing training, and the ethical implications of automated decision-making. By developing an integrated security framework, promoting collaboration, and fostering a culture of continuous improvement, organizations can optimize their cybersecurity efforts and adapt to the ever-changing threat landscape.

As cyber threats become increasingly sophisticated, the synergy between AI and human expertise will be vital in building resilient and adaptive defenses, ultimately safeguarding organizations against the multitude of challenges they face in the digital realm.

12.2 Developing Adaptive and Self-Learning Security Architectures

In today's dynamic cybersecurity landscape, the threats organizations face are becoming increasingly sophisticated and varied. Traditional security architectures, which often rely on static rules and pre-defined responses, struggle to keep pace with the rapid evolution of cyber threats. To address these challenges, the development of adaptive and self-learning security architectures has emerged as a critical approach. This chapter explores the principles, benefits, challenges, and future directions of creating security systems that can evolve and learn over time, ensuring robust protection against an ever-changing threat landscape.

Understanding Adaptive and Self-Learning Security Architectures

Definition and Core Principles

Adaptive and self-learning security architectures are systems designed to automatically adjust their defenses based on real-time threat intelligence, user behavior, and environmental changes. These architectures leverage advanced technologies such as machine learning, artificial intelligence, and big data analytics to create an agile security posture that evolves with emerging threats.

Key Characteristics:

- **Real-time adaptability**: The ability to modify security controls and responses based on current threat landscapes and operational contexts.
- **Continuous learning**: The capacity to analyze past incidents and user behaviors to enhance detection capabilities and refine response strategies.
- **Automated decision-making**: The use of algorithms to autonomously determine the best course of action in response to detected threats.

Components of Adaptive Security Architectures

A successful adaptive security architecture typically comprises several interconnected components that facilitate its dynamic nature:

- **Threat Intelligence Feeds**: Continuous updates on emerging threats, vulnerabilities, and attack trends from various sources, providing essential context for decision-making.
- **Machine Learning Models**: Algorithms that analyze historical data and real-time inputs to identify patterns and anomalies indicative of potential threats.
- **Automated Response Mechanisms**: Systems that can implement immediate responses based on detected anomalies, such as isolating compromised devices or adjusting access controls.

- **Feedback Loops**: Mechanisms that allow for continuous improvement by integrating lessons learned from past incidents into future security operations.

Benefits of Adaptive and Self-Learning Architectures

Enhanced Threat Detection and Response

One of the primary advantages of adaptive security architectures is their ability to improve threat detection and response times. By continuously analyzing data and adjusting defenses, these systems can identify anomalies more effectively and respond to threats in real-time.

Example: If a user's behavior deviates significantly from established patterns, the system can autonomously flag this behavior for investigation and initiate protective measures without human intervention.

Reduced Dependence on Static Rules

Traditional security measures often rely on static rules and signatures, which can be ineffective against new and evolving threats. Adaptive security architectures eliminate the need for constant rule updates by employing self-learning algorithms that can recognize novel attack vectors.

Benefit: This flexibility allows organizations to stay ahead of adversaries who may exploit unknown vulnerabilities.

Improved Resource Allocation

By automating many routine security tasks and providing real-time insights, adaptive security architectures enable organizations to allocate their resources more effectively. Security teams can focus on higher-level strategic initiatives rather than being bogged down by repetitive tasks.

Action Item: This optimized allocation of human resources can lead to more proactive security measures and overall improved security posture.

Greater Resilience Against Advanced Threats

The dynamic nature of adaptive and self-learning architectures equips organizations to better withstand advanced persistent threats (APTs) and sophisticated cyber attacks.

These systems can quickly adjust their defenses in response to real-time intelligence and emerging attack methods.

Example: If an attacker employs a new technique to bypass traditional defenses, a self-learning architecture can analyze the attempt and adjust its protocols accordingly.
Challenges in Developing Adaptive Security Architectures

Complexity of Implementation

Developing and deploying adaptive and self-learning security architectures can be a complex undertaking, requiring significant investment in technology, talent, and processes. Organizations may face challenges in integrating these systems with existing infrastructure and ensuring compatibility.

Concern: A lack of integration can lead to gaps in security coverage and inefficient response protocols.

Data Privacy and Compliance Concerns

As adaptive security architectures often rely on the continuous collection and analysis of vast amounts of data, organizations must navigate data privacy and regulatory compliance challenges. Ensuring that sensitive information is protected and compliant with relevant regulations is crucial.

Recommendation: Implement strong data governance policies and practices to protect user privacy while still leveraging the benefits of data-driven security.

Evolving Threat Landscape

While adaptive security architectures are designed to learn from and respond to threats, they must also contend with the rapidly changing nature of cyber threats. New attack vectors and techniques emerge regularly, which can outpace the learning curve of these systems.

Action Item: Organizations should continuously update their training datasets and model parameters to ensure that self-learning systems remain effective.

Human Oversight and Accountability

As security architectures become increasingly autonomous, the need for human oversight and accountability becomes more critical. Organizations must ensure that decision-making processes remain transparent and that human analysts can intervene when necessary.

Concern: Maintaining a balance between automation and human intervention is essential to avoid potential pitfalls associated with fully automated systems.

Best Practices for Developing Adaptive Security Architectures

Start with a Strong Foundation

Organizations should begin by establishing a solid foundation of security policies, procedures, and technologies. This foundation will support the integration of adaptive and self-learning components and ensure that they align with organizational goals.

Key Components: Include robust threat intelligence capabilities, incident response protocols, and baseline security measures.

Foster a Culture of Collaboration

To maximize the effectiveness of adaptive security architectures, organizations should promote collaboration between IT, security, and business teams. Cross-functional collaboration can facilitate information sharing and ensure that security initiatives align with overall business objectives.

Action Item: Create a culture of communication and knowledge sharing that encourages collaboration among different teams.

Implement Continuous Monitoring and Feedback Loops

Establishing continuous monitoring and feedback mechanisms is essential for maintaining the effectiveness of adaptive security architectures. Organizations should regularly assess the performance of their systems and incorporate lessons learned from past incidents.

Benefit: Continuous monitoring allows for real-time adjustments and improvements to security measures.

Invest in Training and Skill Development

As adaptive security architectures become more prevalent, organizations must invest in training their cybersecurity personnel to effectively leverage these systems. Training should cover the nuances of AI and machine learning, incident response, and data analysis.

Action Item: Develop comprehensive training programs that equip staff with the skills necessary to maximize the benefits of adaptive security technologies.

Establish Clear Governance and Accountability Frameworks

Organizations must create governance frameworks that outline the roles and responsibilities of human analysts and automated systems. This framework should include protocols for addressing errors or unintended consequences resulting from automated decisions.

Recommendation: Clearly define decision-making processes and establish accountability for both human and machine actions.

Future Directions for Adaptive Security Architectures

Integration with Advanced Technologies

The future of adaptive security architectures will likely involve deeper integration with emerging technologies such as quantum computing, blockchain, and Internet of Things (IoT) devices. These advancements can enhance the capabilities of self-learning systems and improve threat detection and response.

Action Item: Organizations should explore partnerships and collaborations with technology providers to stay at the forefront of cybersecurity innovations.

Evolution of Machine Learning Algorithms

As machine learning algorithms continue to advance, adaptive security architectures will benefit from more sophisticated models capable of learning from increasingly complex data sets. These improvements will enhance the accuracy of threat detection and response mechanisms.

Benefit: Enhanced algorithms will enable organizations to better anticipate and mitigate emerging threats.

Focus on User Behavior Analytics

Future developments in adaptive security architectures will likely place greater emphasis on user behavior analytics (UBA). By monitoring user behavior in real time, organizations can detect anomalies and potential insider threats more effectively.

Example: Integrating UBA with self-learning architectures can provide insights into abnormal behaviors that might indicate compromised accounts or insider threats.

Greater Emphasis on Resilience

As the cybersecurity landscape continues to evolve, the focus on resilience will become paramount. Adaptive security architectures will need to incorporate resilience principles that prioritize recovery and continuity in the face of attacks.

Recommendation: Develop strategies that not only focus on prevention but also emphasize the ability to recover quickly from incidents.

Developing adaptive and self-learning security architectures is a vital step toward achieving robust cybersecurity in an increasingly complex threat landscape. By leveraging the capabilities of machine learning, real-time data analysis, and automated decision-making, organizations can create dynamic security systems that evolve alongside emerging threats.

However, the successful implementation of these architectures requires careful consideration of the challenges involved, including complexity, data privacy, and the need for human oversight. By adopting best practices and fostering a culture of collaboration and continuous improvement, organizations can maximize the benefits of adaptive security architectures and build a resilient defense against cyber threats.

As cyber adversaries become more sophisticated, the integration of adaptive and self-learning technologies will be essential for organizations striving to maintain their security posture and safeguard their digital assets in the ever-evolving landscape of cybersecurity.

12.3 The Human-AI Cybersecurity Partnership: Best Practices for Organizations

In the current landscape of cybersecurity, the integration of artificial intelligence (AI) with human expertise is not just beneficial; it is essential. While AI technologies can analyze vast amounts of data, identify patterns, and automate routine tasks, human professionals provide critical thinking, contextual understanding, and ethical reasoning. This chapter explores best practices for organizations seeking to cultivate a productive partnership between AI and human analysts, maximizing the effectiveness of their cybersecurity initiatives.

Understanding the Human-AI Partnership in Cybersecurity

The Complementary Roles of AI and Humans

AI Capabilities:

- **Data Processing**: AI can rapidly analyze large datasets, identifying anomalies and potential threats that might go unnoticed by human analysts.
- **Automation**: By automating repetitive tasks, AI frees human professionals to focus on more complex decision-making and strategic planning.
- **Predictive Analysis**: AI can forecast potential attacks based on historical data and patterns, enabling proactive security measures.

Human Contributions:

- **Contextual Insight**: Humans can interpret complex situations, understanding the broader implications of potential threats and the motivations behind them.
- **Critical Thinking**: Human analysts can evaluate AI-generated insights, making informed decisions based on nuanced understanding rather than relying solely on algorithms.
- **Collaboration**: Humans excel at working in teams, sharing knowledge, and communicating findings effectively across different departments.

The Synergy Between AI and Human Analysts

The optimal approach to cybersecurity lies in leveraging the strengths of both AI and human experts. This partnership fosters a dynamic security environment where rapid data analysis and human intuition work hand-in-hand to respond to threats more effectively.

Example: An AI system may detect a suspicious anomaly in network traffic. Rather than automatically responding, it can alert a human analyst, who can then assess the situation with context and decide whether it warrants further investigation or immediate action.

Best Practices for Fostering a Human-AI Partnership

Establish Clear Communication Channels

Effective communication is crucial for a successful human-AI partnership. Organizations should create platforms for human analysts to interact with AI systems, providing feedback and insights on AI-generated alerts and recommendations.

Action Item: Develop user-friendly interfaces that allow analysts to easily understand and interpret AI findings. Incorporate feedback loops where human analysts can share insights that can be used to improve AI algorithms.

Provide Comprehensive Training Programs

Organizations must invest in training their cybersecurity personnel to work effectively with AI tools. Training should encompass not only technical skills but also critical thinking, data analysis, and ethical considerations related to AI.

Key Components:

- **AI Understanding**: Training programs should educate analysts on how AI works, its limitations, and how to interpret its outputs.
- **Scenario-Based Training**: Conduct exercises that simulate real-world scenarios where AI and human analysts must collaborate to respond to threats.

Create a Culture of Collaboration

Encouraging a collaborative environment where human analysts and AI systems complement each other can enhance the overall security posture of an organization. Foster teamwork between IT, security teams, and business units to break down silos.

Benefit: A culture of collaboration allows for more comprehensive threat assessments and encourages innovative approaches to problem-solving.

Implement Continuous Feedback Mechanisms

Continuous improvement is essential for both AI systems and human analysts. Organizations should establish processes for ongoing feedback to refine AI algorithms and enhance human decision-making.

Action Item: Create a structured system for analysts to provide feedback on AI performance, including false positives, false negatives, and situational context. Use this information to train and optimize AI models continually.

Define Roles and Responsibilities Clearly

To maximize the effectiveness of the human-AI partnership, organizations should clearly define the roles and responsibilities of both AI systems and human analysts. This delineation helps ensure that each party knows its functions within the cybersecurity framework.

Key Considerations:

- **Escalation Procedures**: Establish protocols for when and how AI should escalate issues to human analysts.
- **Human Oversight**: Define situations where human intervention is required, especially in cases where ethical considerations come into play.

Leverage AI for Threat Intelligence Gathering

AI systems can enhance threat intelligence efforts by automating the collection and analysis of data from various sources. By harnessing AI's ability to aggregate and analyze threat data, organizations can equip human analysts with actionable insights.

Action Item: Implement AI tools that monitor global threat landscapes, providing human analysts with up-to-date intelligence on emerging threats and vulnerabilities.

Encourage Innovation and Experimentation

The integration of AI in cybersecurity presents opportunities for innovation. Organizations should foster an environment that encourages experimentation with new AI technologies and methodologies.

Benefit: Embracing a mindset of continuous experimentation allows organizations to stay ahead of evolving threats and explore novel approaches to cybersecurity challenges.

Focus on Ethical Considerations and Bias Mitigation

As AI systems become more prevalent in cybersecurity, organizations must address ethical implications and the potential for algorithmic bias. It's vital to ensure that AI decisions are transparent, fair, and do not disproportionately impact certain user groups.

Action Item: Implement frameworks for evaluating and mitigating bias in AI algorithms. Involve human analysts in assessing AI outputs to ensure ethical considerations are prioritized.

Challenges in Implementing a Human-AI Partnership

Resistance to Change

One of the most significant barriers to integrating AI into cybersecurity processes is resistance from human analysts who may fear that AI will replace their roles. Addressing this fear requires effective communication about the complementary nature of the partnership.

Recommendation: Highlight success stories where AI has enhanced human capabilities rather than replaced them, reinforcing the message that AI is a tool for empowerment.

Skill Gaps and Training Needs

The rapid pace of AI advancements can create skill gaps among human analysts. Organizations must be proactive in identifying training needs and providing resources for continuous learning.

Action Item: Conduct regular assessments of analysts' skills and knowledge regarding AI technologies, adjusting training programs accordingly.

Complexity of AI Systems

The complexity of AI algorithms can make them difficult for human analysts to understand fully. Ensuring that analysts can interpret AI outputs accurately is crucial for effective decision-making.

Benefit: Organizations should prioritize transparency in AI processes, providing training and resources to help analysts understand how AI arrives at its conclusions.

Case Studies of Successful Human-AI Partnerships

Incident Response Teams

Many organizations have successfully implemented AI-powered tools in their incident response teams. For instance, a leading financial institution utilized AI-driven analytics to monitor transactions for fraudulent activity. Human analysts reviewed flagged transactions, allowing the institution to respond to threats swiftly and effectively.

Outcome: This partnership reduced the time taken to detect and respond to potential fraud by over 40%, demonstrating the power of collaboration between AI and human expertise.

Threat Intelligence Platforms

Some companies have integrated AI into their threat intelligence platforms, enabling analysts to receive automated insights into potential threats. In one case, a tech company used AI to analyze threat data from various sources, which human analysts then contextualized within the company's operational environment.

Outcome: This collaboration allowed the organization to prioritize threats more effectively and allocate resources where they were needed most.

Phishing Detection Systems

AI has been instrumental in improving phishing detection capabilities. Organizations have implemented AI-driven systems that analyze email content for signs of phishing attacks. Human analysts review flagged emails, using their contextual knowledge to make final determinations.

Outcome: This partnership led to a significant reduction in successful phishing attacks, as human analysts could intervene before users were exposed to threats.

The partnership between human analysts and AI technologies is essential for effective cybersecurity in today's complex threat landscape. By fostering a collaborative environment, organizations can leverage the strengths of both AI and human expertise, enhancing their ability to detect, respond to, and mitigate cyber threats.

Implementing best practices, such as clear communication, comprehensive training, and continuous feedback, will enable organizations to create a resilient cybersecurity framework that adapts to evolving challenges. As the field of cybersecurity continues to evolve, the human-AI partnership will play a pivotal role in shaping the future of digital defense. Organizations that embrace this partnership will be better positioned to protect their assets and respond effectively to the growing array of cyber threats.

In **AI and Cybersecurity: A Symbiotic Defense System**, *Artyom Ivanov* takes readers on a comprehensive journey into the dynamic world of artificial intelligence and its transformative role in cybersecurity. As cyber threats grow in scale and complexity, traditional methods of defense are no longer sufficient. AI, with its ability to detect, analyze, and respond to cyberattacks in real-time, is reshaping the future of digital security.

This book delves into how AI-driven technologies are revolutionizing threat detection, incident response, and risk mitigation across industries. It explores the deep integration of AI in security operations, from machine learning models that predict future attacks to natural language processing (NLP) tools that combat phishing and social engineering. It also uncovers the emerging risks posed by AI weaponization, such as adversarial machine learning, and how defenders can stay ahead in the arms race against AI-powered cybercrime.

Packed with real-world examples, practical insights, and forward-looking predictions, AI and Cybersecurity provides a roadmap for businesses, security professionals, and tech enthusiasts to navigate the rapidly evolving cybersecurity landscape. It highlights the ethical challenges, the need for collaboration between humans and AI, and the future possibilities that self-learning, autonomous defense systems may unlock.

Whether you're a cybersecurity veteran or new to the field, this book offers invaluable insights into how AI and cybersecurity are merging into a symbiotic force to protect our increasingly digital world.

www.ingramcontent.com/pod-product-compliance
Lightning Source LLC
Chambersburg PA
CBHW062104220526
45471CB00010B/3592